MAJOR GENERAL BENJAMIN D. FOULOIS, USAF, RETIRED, BY ROBERT PHILLIP
General Foulois, still active at the age of 86 as an aviation lecturer and director of the Air
Force Historical Foundation, enlisted in the Army Corps of Engineers in 1898. Commissioned
in 1901, he was Chief of the Air Service, American Expeditionary Force, in World War I. He
served as Chief of the Air Corps from 1931 to 1935 and retired on December 31, 1935. In 1964,
he was awarded a special Congressional Medal of Recognition ''for more than 50 years of
dedication and service to the development of aviation.''

# View of a Great Saga

It is with great pride and pleasure that I introduce and recommend this volume, which tells the dramatic story of the growth and accomplishments of the United States Air Force in minimal text and maximal visibility.

Since 1907 my business has been aviation; in particular, aviation as utilized by the USAF and its predecessor organizations. I lay no claim to expertise in the field of art, but it occurs to me that there are similarities between art and the profession of flying. Each demands talent and training, intellect and imagination, a clear eye and a steady hand. I admire the skill behind the art work contained herein as I admire the effortless flying of a practiced airman.

I am thoroughly familiar with the colorful history of our Air Force, but this book presents a new and exciting view of a great saga. The crisp text provides an effective backdrop for the excellent art and the expressive brushes of the artists lend an added dimension of depth. I think that the unique format of this volume will bring to its reader a greater appreciation of what the Air Force is and what it means to the nation.

— *Major General Benjamin Foulois, Former Chief of the Army Air Corps*  v

# *Acknowledgements*

The preparation of this volume entailed a dual line of effort: one in historical research; the other in a detailed study of the Air Force Art Collection. The task required the cooperation of a number of past and present members of the United States Air Force, to whom the authors and the publisher are deeply indebted.

Particular mention must be made of the tireless and patient aid provided by Major Lloyd M. Peterson, Assistant Chief, Art and Museum Branch, Office of Information, Department of the Air Force. The project also benefited from the work of William H. Winder and Mrs. Leora M. Stanley of the Art and Museum Branch.

The authors further express their gratitude to Lieutenant Colonel William J. Lookadoo, USAF, Office of Information, for his assistance in several phases of the project; Lieutenant Colonel Gene Gurney, USAF, Department of Defense Magazine and Book Branch, who provided the initial impetus; and to noted air historian Colonel Samuel Taylor Moore, USAF Retired, who made available material from his research files.

Other contributors of time, advice, encouragement and information include Major General E. B. LeBailly, USAF, Director of Information, and his former deputy, Brigadier General Maurice Casey, USAF; Colonel Roger Payne, USAF, Director of Information Services, Headquarters Command, and his deputy, Captain Bonnie O'Leary, WAF; Colonel Dwight R. Dinsmore, USAF, Deputy Chief of the Public Information Division, Office of Information, Department of the Air Force; and Mr. David Shoem, USAF Historical Division, who conducted an accuracy check of the text content.

To all of the above, the authors tender their thanks and sincere appreciation.

*James J. Haggerty*
*Warren Reiland Smith*

*The* U.S. Air Force: *A Pictorial History in Art*

# The U.S

*A Spartan Boo*

# AIR FORCE:

# *A Pictorial*

# *History in Art*

*by* James J. Haggerty *and* Warren Reiland Smith

BOOKS, INC., *Publishers* · New York and Washington, D. C.

Library of Congress Catalog Card No. 65-28296

*Printed in the United States of America*

# The Air Force Documentary Art Program

The practice of documenting military operations by means of art is centuries old. In the United States, it may be traced to the latter part of the 18th century, when the colonies were engaged in a battle for independence under General George Washington. One of the first military painters was John Trumbull, a member of Washington's staff who later became an important artist in early Americana.

The availability of the camera made possible greater documentation of military operations in war and peace, but there was still a need for the special talents of the artist in establishing official visual records. The French government formally recognized the extra dimension a painter brings to the visual record during World War I, when it commissioned Henri Farré to depict on canvas the history-making accomplishments of the Flying Corps.

In World War II, Frank E. Beresford, an eminent British artist and war correspondent, spent more than three years at various bases painting the activities of the United States Army Air Forces. A number of other artists similarly documented the role of the Army's pilots and crewmen during this period.

Soon after the Air Force became a separate service in 1947, the USAF received from the Army more than 500 combat art paintings of World War II. These, together with the Farré collection of 68 paintings and the Beresford collection of 50 paintings donated to the Air Force Art Collection, form a valuable historical record of the activities of the air service in the first half of this century.

In 1951, the Air Force took 90 of America's most famous illustrators and editorial cartoonists on an indoctrination tour of USAF installations. Their escort officer on that trip, Lieutenant Colonel William J. Lookadoo, conceived the idea of a permanent USAF art program whereby noted illustrators would record the contemporary Air Force story. With the concurrence of Major General Sory Smith, then Director of Information for the USAF, Colonel Lookadoo met with the Board of Governors of the Society of Illustrators of New York in April, 1954, and extended an invitation for their participation in the program.

Since a great many of the Society's members had been active on the battle fronts of World War I and World War II, the invitation was enthusiastically accepted. The program machinery was set up in the same year by Lieutenant Colonel George C. Bales, an Air Force officer who was also an artist and a member of the Society of Illustrators of New York. Colonel Bales became Director of Art, USAF, and he brought into the new program the Societies of Illustrators of Los Angeles and San Francisco as well as the New York group. In October, 1963, he was succeeded as USAF art director by Major Lloyd M. Peterson, and in October, 1965, the USAF created a new Art and Museum Branch, headed by Major John Devoe and Major Peterson.

The three societies have presented to the Air Force more than 800 paintings, and a number of other artists have given their time and talent to document the aerospace history of the United States. The Air Force Art Collection continues to grow in size and significance, and it now numbers more than 2,500 paintings and drawings. This art hangs regularly in the corridors of the Pentagon; in the galleries of the Air Force Museum at Wright-Patterson Air Force Base, Dayton, Ohio; at the United States Air Force Academy, Colorado Springs, Colorado; in the library at the Air University, Maxwell Air Force Base, Alabama; and in the White House. In addition, art is circulated by van to selected cities in the United States and the paintings and drawings have been exhibited in museums and educational and cultural centers throughout the United States and the Far East.

The art reproduced in this volume represents only a small portion of the collection, but it provides an excellent cross-section of the type of work contributed by the illustrators. Artists whose paintings are included herein are:

Al Avison; George C. Bales; James Bama; Charles Baskerville; C. C. Beall; Francis Henry Beaugureau; Bill Bender; Frank E. Beresford; Roy Besser; Neil Boyle; Gerald Brockhurst; Carl Broemel; Marbury Hill Brown; Reynold Brown; Lynn Buckham; Al Buell; Paul Callé; Collin Bruce Campbell; Joseph Cleary; Chet Collom; Mario Cooper; Donald V. Crowley; Al Dempster; Dean Ellis; Henri Farré; Dean (William) Fausett; Nicolai Fechin; Keith Ferris; Loren Fisher; Stanley W. Galli; Nixon Galloway; Robert Geissmann; Frank Germain; Richard Green; Bob Greenberg; Earl G. Gross; John Groth; David Hall; Robert Handville; Lloyd F. Harting; Peter Hurd; Ralph Iligan; Woodi Ishmael; Harvey Kidder; Warren King; David Klein; Sandor Klein; Clayton Knight; Alexander Kortner; Charles J. Kuderna; Robert H. Laessig; John Lavalle; Robert Lavin; Jack Levine; Milton Marx; Tran Mawicke; Robert T. McCall; Gerald McConnell; John T. McCoy; Wesley B. McKeown; Sam McKim; Si Mezerow; Herb Mott; Alfred Muenchen; Norman Nicholson; Robert Phillip; Barye W. Phillips; John Pike; Ogden Pleissner; Robert Poole; Ray Prohaska; Noel Quinn; Walter Richards; Art Riley, Harry J. Schaare; John Scott; Carl Setterberg; George A. Shealy; Harrison Standley; Thomas Edgar Stephens; Paul Trebilcock; Thornton Utz; Elin Waite; Robert O. Watkins; Ren Wicks.

Biographies of these artists will be found on page 247.

# Contents

# CHAPTER I

# The Fledgling Years

*Genesis at Kitty Hawk*

The United States Air Force has had many names and many birthdays. It has existed under its present title since September 18, 1947, when the National Defense Act created an air arm of independent status, co-equal with the Army and the Navy. But this was simply a change in the formal structure of the national defense system. The Air Force is more than an organizational entity; it is men, machines, purpose and tradition. In ever-increasing degree of importance to the nation's welfare, it has been an integral part of the military services since the early years of this century.

From the time of the Civil War, military men had ventured into the air in captive and free balloons. The balloon's function in military operations, however, was limited; it was confined to observation of enemy troop dispositions and air-directed regulation of artillery fire. The real genesis of air power awaited development of the far more flexible heavier-than-air flying machine. That became a reality on December 17, 1903, when Orville Wright lifted his frail 12-horsepower *Flyer* off the sands of Kill Devil Hills near Kitty Hawk, North Carolina.

Several years were to elapse, however, before the airplane found its way into military service. In 1904-05, the Wrights tried without success to interest both the U.S. and British governments. But by 1907, there were a few visionaries who had grasped the significance of the Wrights' achievement, and the Aero Club of America prevailed upon President Theodore Roosevelt to investigate the defense potential of the flying machine.

On August 1, 1907, the War Department created the forerunner of the modern Air Force: the Aeronautical Division in the Office of the Chief Signal Officer of the Army. Captain Charles deForrest Chandler was assigned to head the division and given a staff of two enlisted men and a civilian clerk. Emphasis in the division was to be on balloons and dirigible airships, but the first evidence of awakening military interest in heavier-than-air craft was contained in the memorandum creating Captain Chandler's command: ''This division will have charge of all matters pertaining to military ballooning, air machines and all kindred subjects.'' The seeds planted by Orville and Wilbur Wright in 1903 were beginning to germinate.

2

*THE WRIGHT BROTHERS' FIRST POWERED FLIGHT,
BY HARVEY KIDDER.*

*Triumph and Tragedy*

The President's instructions to the War Department to explore the potential of the flying machine resulted in a detailed investigation by the Army's Board of Ordnance and Fortification, culminating late in 1907 with Wilbur Wright's personal appearance before the Board. Citing his own and his brother's extensive flying experience, the elder Wright convinced the Board members that he could provide an airplane capable of meeting specifications drawn up by the Aeronautical Division. On February 10, 1908, the Army signed a contract with the Wrights for delivery of the first signal Corps airplane.

Specifications called for a machine that could carry two persons in sitting positions, rather than one in a prone position as had been the case in the original Flyer. The plane would have to have a speed of at least 40 miles per hour, a range of 125 miles and a flight duration of not less than one hour.

The Wrights completed the airplane in just six months and delivered it to Fort Myer, Virginia, on August 10, 1908. Wilbur had gone to France to make a series of public flights with another machine, so it fell to Orville to make the Army demonstrations. On September 9, before a crowd of hundreds, Orville made the first flight in history of more than one hour's duration. On the same afternoon, Lieutenant Frank P. Lahm, the second officer assigned to the Aeronautical Division, became the first military man to fly as a passenger in a heavier-than-air vehicle.

With President Taft and a number of cabinet members in frequent attendance, Orville Wright successfully continued his demonstrations for another week. Then, on September 17, tragedy struck.

One of the observers at the trials was Lieutenant Thomas E. Selfridge, who had flown gliders and who had designed the first airplane for civilian Aerial Experiment Association. On the fateful 17th of September, Selfridge accepted Orville Wright's invitation to fly as a passenger. On a turn over Fort Myer at an altitude of 150 feet, one of the pusher propellers struck a diagonal bracing wire. The propeller snapped, the machine went out of control and crashed.

Both Wright and Selfridge were rushed to the post hospital, where Lieutenant Selfridge died a few hours later, the first fatality of powered flight. Orville Wright survived the crash, but he was hospitalized for seven weeks.

Thus, within a single week, the fledging air service has seen the first military passengers take to the air and suffered its first casualty. The triumphs outweighed the tragedy; the War Department representatives were sufficiently impressed by the success prior to the accident to grant the Wrights an extension of the acceptance period until the summer of 1909.

LIEUTENANT LAHM'S FIRST FLIGHT, BY RICHARD GREEN.
On September 9, 1908, Frank P. Lahm became the first military passenger when
he went aloft with Orville Wright during the Fort Myer trials. Earlier in the
year, Lieutenant Thomas E. Selfridge had become the first military soloist.

*Airplane Number One Accepted*

On June 20, 1909, Orville Wright returned to Fort Myer to resume the qualification tests, this time accompanied by his brother. Wilbur, however, was to be only a back-up pilot; Orville wanted to finish what he had started.

During the winter, the Wrights had been busy building a new airplane, incorporating structural changes to prevent propeller fouling by the bracing wires and improvements to provide additional speed.

After a month of "warm-up" flights, the official trials in the presence of the Aeronautical Board got under way. On July 27, Orville and his machine easily met the two-man duration requirement of one hour. Carrying Lieutenant Lahm as passenger, he flew for one hour, 12 minutes and 40 seconds, a record for two-man flight.

For the speed trials, the Aeronautical Board had laid out a cross-country route from Fort Myer to Shooters Hill in Alexandria, Virginia, where a captive balloon served as a pylon, and then back to Fort Myer. On July 30, before some 7,000 spectators, Orville took off from Fort Myer with Lieutenant Benjamin D. Foulois, a member of the Board, as his passenger.

At altitudes at times topping 400 feet, an exceptional height, Wright and Foulois sped the three miles to the pylon in slightly over four minutes, made the turn and started back. The crowd at Fort Myer tensed as the airplane disappeared from sight between two ridges, but in a moment it reappeared and flew directly over the finish line. The ovation from the spectators was thunderous, loud enough to be heard by the two airmen over the noise of the engine.

The timers quickly computed the speed, an average of 42.583 miles per hour, well over the requirement and good enough to earn the Wrights a bonus of 5,000 dollars in addition to the base contract price of 25,000 dollars for their machine. The airplane was accepted and military aviation was on its way.

There remained one other contractual specification: the Wrights had to train two military pilots. Lieutenants Lahm and Foulois were selected, but the latter was designated to attend an aeronautical conference in France and he was replaced by Lieutenant Frederic E. Humphreys, detached from the Corps of Engineers. After his return from Europe, Foulois managed to get three hours of flight instruction from Wilbur Wright and some additional tutelage from Humphreys, the first military flight instructor.

THE WRIGHT BROTHERS AT FORT MYER, BY JOHN McCOY.

*College Park and Fort Sam Houston*

While the trials at Fort Myer were under way, the Signal Corps decided it needed a new and roomier airfield, so a search for a new site was instigated. After a series of aerial observations by means of free balloon ascensions, the Aeronautical Division selected an open field at College Park, Maryland, near what is now the University of Maryland but in 1909 was the Maryland Agricultural College. It was here that Lieutenants Lahm and Humphreys made the first military solo flights on October 26, 1909, with Humphreys preceding Lahm by a few minutes.

It was also at College Park, on November 3, 1909, that Lieutenant Lahm carried his first passenger, Lieutenant George C. Sweet, USN, who thus became the first Navy officer to fly in an airplane.

Shortly after that flight, the Chief Signal Officer decided that the strong winds prevalent in the College Park area during the winter made it advisable to set up a new field in the southern United States for winter operations. Fort Sam Houston, near San Antonio, Texas, was selected and arrangements were made to ship the lone airplane and its crew to the new location.

At the start of 1910, the embryo air service had one administrative officer, three flying officers, nine enlisted men and one civilian mechanic; the equipment inventory included, in addition to the Wright plane, Dirigible No. 1, purchased in 1908, and three balloons. But early in the year, the Division suffered a twin setback. A technicality decreed that Lieutenant Lahm return to troop duty with the calvary and the Corps of Engineers recalled Lieutenant Humphreys. The officer complement was reduced to Captain Chandler, a skilled balloonist who had had no airplane instruction as yet, and Lieutenant Foulois, who had only a few hours of dual flight. The latter completed his training by correspondence course with Wilbur Wright, after making his first solo flight on March 2, 1910, at Fort Sam Houston. He then made some 61 practice flights, logging 9 hours of flight time.

On March 3, the Aeronautical Division received the first appropriation of funds specifically earmarked for aeronautics. With 125,000 dollars available for the fiscal year 1912, the Chief Signal Officer immediately placed orders for five new airplanes—three Wright Type B's and two Curtiss tractor-type biplanes—at a cost of 5,000 dollars each. Another portion of the money was allocated for activation of an aviation school at College Park.

*THE ENTIRE AIR FORCE, 1910, BY RICHARD GREEN.*
*Green's painting shows the Aeronautical Division's first airplane and its crew; rear row, left to right, Private William C. Abolin, a Private Kinsey, Private Glenn R. Madole, Lieutenant Benjamin D. Foulois, and O. G. Simmons, a civilian aero mechanic. Front row, Sergeant Herbert Marcus, Corporal Vernon L. Burge, Private R. W. Brown, Sergeant Stephen J. Idzorek and Private Felix Clarke.*

*Military Tests, A New Name*

During 1911 and 1912, aviation activity heightened at College Park and at a new summer base at Augusta, Georgia. Two new pilot trainees—Lieutenants Henry H. Arnold and Thomas DeWitt Milling —were assigned to the division and sent to the Wright Company's flying school at Dayton, Ohio. On their return to College Park at mid-year of 1911, they joined Chandler, now a flyer, and Foulois in a series of experiments to evaluate the military potential of the airplane.

Arnold and Chandler conducted the first ''long'' cross-country flight from College Park to Frederick, Maryland, on August 21, 1911. During the same month, Milling ran a number of tests of a bombsight invented by Riley Scott, a former Coast Artillery officer. Early in 1912, Foulois experimented with aerial telegraph by means of a small, battery-powered radio transmitter. On June 7 of that year Chandler and Milling teamed to make the first test-firing of a machine gun from an airplane. By the end of 1912, there were 14 flying officers on duty at College Park.

In the following February the College Park station was abandoned in favor of a new school at Texas City, Texas, where aviation experimenters could be closer to troop concentrations for practice in coordinated air-ground maneuvers. Within the next four months, two additional schools were opened, in the Philippines and Hawaii. The tiny air force was growing; it now had 15 planes, 23 officers and 91 enlisted men.

March, 1913, saw the formation of the first U.S. tactical aviation unit. Called the First Aero Squadron and based at North Island, San Diego, California, it was assigned nine officers, 51 enlisted men and nine airplanes.

During 1913, several bills had been introduced in Congress seeking to elevate the Aeronautical Division to branch status on a level with the Signal Corps. Opposition was violent on the part of testifying Signal Corps officers, and a compromise bill was passed. On July 18, 1914, Congress created the Aviation Section, still subordinate to the Signal Corps, with an authorized strength of 60 officers and 260 enlisted men. A sum of 600,000 dollars was appropriated for aeronautical development and Army aviation underwent a period of rapid expansion.

*COLLEGE PARK, BY JOHN McCOY. Lieutenants H. H. Arnold and Thomas DeW. Milling and the Wright Model B at the Aeronautical Division's Maryland training field, circa 1912.*

The next two years saw Europe aflame with war, and the threat of the conflagration's extension to the United States accelerated aviation research. The Aviation Section conducted tests of parachutes, new bombing techniques, spotting of underwater mines, new types of propellers and air-ground liaison with smoke bombs, Very pistols and radio-telegraphy serving as the means of communication.

In 1916, the Aviation Section got its first taste of action—not in Europe, but on the U.S. punitive expedition to Mexico. America's first ''combat'' air operation was a dismal failure.

That March, the First Aero Squadron was ordered to Columbus, New Mexico. Its commanding officer, Benjamin D. Foulois, now a captain, had with him 11 officers, 82 enlisted men and eight airplanes of questionable serviceability. The first mission for the squadron was to fly to the Mexican city of Casas Grandes. It was a preview of what was to come. One plane had an engine failure and turned back to Columbus; a second cracked up on landing, two other pilots became lost; and the remaining four were forced down short of their destination by darkness.

For about a month, the squadron served in the border area, carrying dispatches and scouting for enemy troops. But gusty winds, dust storms and the Mexican mountains combined to defeat the squadron's frail and underpowered aircraft, and crack-ups were frequent. Six of the eight planes were destroyed or abandoned and the other two were so badly battered they had to be condemned. The golden promise of air power had become badly tarnished.

The abortive operation did, however, bring to the attention of the Congress the need for better aircraft and it brought an air appropriation of 13,000,000 dollars for expansion and modernization of the service.

On May 20, 1916, Lieutenant Colonel George O. Squier took command of the Aviation Section. A field officers' course in aeronautics was established at North Island, San Diego, and other schools were opened at Chicago, Memphis and Mineola, New York. In addition, a number of civilian flying schools were given contracts to train Army pilots.

The National Defense Act of 1916 increased the authorized strength of the air arm to 148 flying officers, but at the time the act was passed the U.S. entry into the war was only nine months away and the Aviation Section had only 61 officers and 248 enlisted men. That June 2, the Aviation Section became the Airplane Division of the Signal Corps and Foulois, now a Major, was named officer in-charge.

*NORTH ISLAND, 1916, BY JOHN McCOY.*

*Girding For War*

April 6, 1917, was the date that the United States entered what was later to be known as World War I. In what was to be the pattern for future wars, the air service was completely unprepared. The Airplane Division had 131 officers and slightly more than 1,000 enlisted men in a force several times larger than the previous year's. But the attempted expansion of 1916 had been a case of too little, too late; only 78 of the officers had had flight training, and none had sufficient experience for combat. On paper there were seven squadrons, but none had achieved a state of war readiness and two were only partially organized. There were 55 aircraft, all of them totally unsuited for battle.

The U.S. government instituted a massive air training and aircraft production program, calling for 5,000 pilots, 50,000 ground personnel and 345 air squadrons as well as the manufacture of 21,900 planes for use by the U.S. and Allied forces. Congress appropriated 640,000,000 dollars for the air mobilization task, and the act was signed by President Wilson on 24 July, 1917.

The program, however, was one born of over-optimism and lack of realization of the enormity of the job. There was practically no aviation industry; only 142 planes had been delivered to the Army since the acceptance of the first military aircraft. There were only a handful of companies capable of anything that could be termed *aircraft production*; in fact, some enthusiastic volunteers for manufacturing work in the 1916 expansion had been forced to request release from their Army contracts because of inability to meet their assignments. Moreover, there were few training facilities in the United States.

The infant aircraft industry, nonetheless gave the task its best effort. The decision was to concentrate on producing a few types of existing and reliable aircraft, most of them foreign: the Curtiss JN-4D ''Jenny,'' which was to become the standard training plane; the British DeHavilland-4 and Handley Page 0/400 bombers; and the Italian Caproni bomber. The U.S. would also mass produce its greatest contribution to the air war—the 400-horsepower Liberty engine.

American flying units began arriving in France in the fall of 1917. The First Aero Squadron, now commanded by Major Ralph Royce, reached France on September 3, followed soon after by eight other squadrons and balloon companies. There were no American-built planes available, so U.S. pilots flew French aircraft, taking combat training at Amanty and Epiez under the tutelage of war-experienced French pilots. With the arrival of the First Aero Squadron, Army overseas aviation acquired a new designation: the *Air Service of the American Expeditionary Force.*

*AIRFIELD OF THE 1ST BOMBARDMENT GROUP, MALZEVILLE, FRANCE, 1916, BY HENRI FARRÉ. Many American airmen flew with French and British forces prior to the entry of the United States into World War I.*

*Early Combat*

Several months elapsed between the American airmen's arrival in Europe and their introduction to air combat. During the winter, some 2,500 U.S. pilots received advanced training, most of them in France but about 100 in Italy.

Although a number of American pilots had seen combat action with Allied air units, the Air Service's introduction to the war did not come until March, 1918. The First Aero Squadron was attacked by German planes during a reconnaissance mission but neither side lost an airplane during the engagement.

Two days later, Americans scored their first aerial victories. In a battle over the airdrome at Toul, Lieutenants Alan F. Winslow and Douglas Campbell each shot down an enemy plane.

On June 12, the 96th Aero Squadron entered the air war with a daylight bombing mission against the railroad yards at Dommary-Baroncourt, near Metz. The results were termed highly successful. The 96th continued daylight bombing for the next month, but losses were heavy and on July 10, the squadron, reduced to one airplane, temporarily discontinued operations.

In the meantime, American pilots had started flying with Italian air squadrons. Using the three-engined Italian Caproni bombers, they flew their first mission on June 20.

By July, U.S. air units were reorganized as a brigade and assigned a sector in the Chateau-Thierry area. Commander of the brigade was Colonel William Mitchell, destined to become one of the great and controversial figures of American air history. The son of Senator John Mitchell of Wisconsin, ''Billy'' Mitchell had enlisted as a private with the First Wisconsin Volunteer Regiment in the Spanish-American War. Later he was commissioned a second lieutenant in a signal company. As a Signal Corps captain, he was assigned to the Aviation Section in 1915 as deputy to Colonel Squier, although he did not become a qualified aviator until 1917. Before the United States' entry into the war, Mitchell had been sent to France as an aeronautical observer with the British and French forces, and it was in this capacity that he became the first American military man to fly behind enemy lines.

*AIR BATTLE, 1917, BY HENRI FARRÉ.*

*Success at Saint-Mihiel*

It was not until the closing months of World War I that America's real aerial offensive started. In September, 1918, the Allies initiated a massive drive against German strong points around Saint-Mihiel. The Allies assembled a mighty air force under the command of Billy Mitchell to support the ground movement. The fleet consisted of 1,481 airplanes manned by American, British and French pilots and crews. Some 700 of the planes were fighters, the remainder bombers and observation craft.

Mitchell, already a dedicated proponent of strategic bombing, proceeded to demonstrate the power of the airplane as a strategic weapon in a series of attacks on German railways centers, communications, supply centers and troop concentrations. He also devoted a considerable portion of his force to ''facilitating the advance of ground troops,'' a tactical mission in which he employed his aircraft for observation, photography, direction of artillery fire and strafing ground targets. A third segment of the allied air force concentrated on air superiority, seeking out and engaging enemy planes in an effort to further reduce the dwindling German fighter strength.

In the Saint-Mihiel offensive, the German air force found itself outnumbered for the first time and Mitchell's forces quickly gained air superiority. Behind-the-lines bombing and tactical support missions also proved highly effective. General John J. Pershing, commander of the AEF, was enthusiastic about the performance of the Air Service, and this prompted Major General Mason Patrick, now chief of the AEF's Air Service, to recommend Mitchell's promotion to brigadier general.

In late September and early October, the Germans launched a final counterattack in the Meuse-Argonne area. To assist ground forces in repelling the attack, the Air Service launched, on October 9, the greatest single raid of the war against enemy troop concentrations. More than 200 bombers, escorted by 100 fighters, dropped 30 tons of bombs and knocked down a dozen German aircraft, helping smash the counterattack. On this mission, the bombs were released electrically from mounts beneath the fuselage —a marked advance over the usual technique in which bombardiers had dropped the bombs from the cockpit by guesswork.

Five weeks later, the war was over. Left unfulfilled were Mitchell's proposals to conduct long-range bombardment of German cities deep within the homeland and to parachute large numbers of troops behind enemy lines.

*AEROPLANE FLIGHT OVER THE VERDUN FRONT, BY HENRI FARRÉ.*

*The Knights of the Air*

To the roster of military air pioneers, World War I added a new group of illustrious names: Billy Mitchell, whose vigorous championship of strategic bombing and demonstration of its effectiveness laid the groundwork for future development of this vital air role; Mason Patrick, who provided the Air Service of the AEF with efficient and sorely needed management; and there were the "aces," a new breed of men whose daring exploits captured the fancy of the public and brought support for post-war continuance of aviation as an integral part of military operations.

An ace was one who shot down five or more enemy aircraft or balloons. There were many who achieved such status, but among the more prominent were Captain Elliott White Springs, who scored 12 victories; Major George A. Vaughn, with 13; and Major Raoul Lufberry, with 17.

One of the greatest of the allied aces was Lieutenant Frank J. Luke, the "balloon buster." Within a period of two weeks in September, 1918, Luke destroyed 14 balloons and shot down four enemy planes in dog-fights. On five occasions he flew back to base in a plane so badly damaged it had to be condemned.

On one occasion, Luke attacked and destroyed three more balloons. Although badly wounded in the action, he flew on to the village of Murvaux and strafed a German troop concentration. Forced down, either from weakness or damage to his plane, Luke refused to surrender to a German squad and opened fire with his pistol. The Germans returned the fire and Luke was killed. Frank Luke received a posthumous Medal of Honor, becoming the only member of the Air Service to be so honored while the war was in progress.

Finally, there was the most victorious of all the American aces, Lieutenant Eddie Rickenbacker. "Rick," a former auto racing driver who had gone to France as chauffeur to General Pershing, joined the 94th Aero Squadron and scored his first kill on April 29, 1918. He added five more during the month of May before an ear infection grounded him for three months. In September he returned to combat and over the next two months he notched an additional 20 victories to end the war with a total of 26, the best record compiled by an American flyer.

*Armistice and a Concept Acknowledged*

At the Armistice on November 11, 1918, the Air Service consisted of 45 squadrons with 767 pilots, 504 observiers and gunners and 740 airplanes assigned to the various armies. The American air strength was a far cry from the 263 squadrons promised 18 months earlier; nor had the home front come anywhere near the grandiose plan for delivery of more than 20,000 aircraft to the allies. Some American-built planes reached Europe, but they came in crates and needed a long period of assembly and tests before they could be placed in service. The war ended before any American plane was ready for combat duty.

But the young air arm had written a glowing chapter in the annals of air power. Despite a late start, U.S. aviators had flown more than 35,000 combat hours; they had made some 13,000 pursuit flights, 6,600 observation missions and about 1,100 bombardment sorties. They had dropped on the enemy about 276,000 pounds of explosives, a puny figure by modern standards but an impressive one in light of the planes then available. They had destroyed 781 enemy aircraft and 73 balloons while suffering losses of 289 planes and 49 balloons.

There were no claims that air power had won the war; had there been, they would have been completely unjustified. It was the infantry soldier's war, in which advantage was eked out yard by yard, and the primary assistance came not from the air, but from the artillery. Tactical air operations were limited by the vulnerability of the flimsy aircraft to fire from the ground, bombing missions by the relatively short range of the planes available.

Incontestably, however, the Air Service made a substantial contribution to the overall Allied effort. If it was not a dominant force in the war, it was at least an important adjunct. In its first real combat operations, the Air Service, together with the flying forces of the other nations, had demonstrated that defense was no longer the sole province of ships on the seas or armies on the ground. To the grim business of war, a new dimension had been added.

Less than a decade had passed since the Army had accepted its first airplane. Many more years were to pass before the air force reached maturity. But the action in Europe's skies had proved that the Air Service had a definite place in the nation's defense structure.

# CHAPTER II

# The Adolescent Years

*The Ostfriesland Incident*

With the end of the war, the Air Service was hard put to justify its existence. Army pilots were flying the airmail but under Post Office jurisdiction. One peacetime application of aviation was found in 1919: the use of aerial patrols for the prevention of forest fires. To many who had fought in France, however, air power had a greater destiny than fire-spotting. An outspoken group, led by Generals Foulois and Mitchell, wanted recognition of the potential of the airplane and a separate air arm.

They lost the initial battle. On June 4, 1920, Congress passed an Army reorganization act which made a permanent Air Service but only as ''a coordinate branch of the line of the Army." The new Service was organized into two wings—one at Langley Field, Virginia, the other at Kelly Field, Texas. The wings embraced seven groups—four within the United States and two outside—and the authorized strength was set at 1,516 officers and 16,000 enlisted men.

Advocating development of strategic bombing techniques and use of aircraft as coastal defense weapons, stormy, flamboyant Billy Mitchell carried the fight for air power to the Congress and to the American people, initiating a bitter controversy among Army and Navy officers and their civilian leadership. Although some naval officers firmly believed in the potential of the airplane, they saw it as a carrier-based rather than a land-based weapon. Mitchell, now Assistant Chief of the Air Service, touched off a feud with the Navy by stating publicly that sea power was obsolete and that his bombers could sink the biggest surface vessels. His insistent, widely publicized demands for a chance to prove his theories led to a joint Army-Navy series of tests in June and July, 1921.

The highlight of these tests, which included finding and bombing surface vessels by both Army and Navy aircraft, was an attack on the captured German battleship *Ostfriesland.* Armed with live 2,000-pound bombs, seven Martin MB-2 bombers under Mitchell's direction flew from Langley Field on July 21 to a point 60 miles off the Virginia coast, where the great German ship was anchored. The Air Service pilots scored some direct hits and some equally devastating bursts close to the hull and sank the *Ostfriesland* in twenty-one minutes.

It should have been a great victory for Mitchell, and it did bring a modicum of public support. But the Navy pointed out that the German battleship had been at anchor, unmanned and unarmed. Mitchell counter-argued that the ship would have been an easier target had it been under way and that it would have sunk more quickly had its magazines been full. The argument as to air power's place in defense continued to rage.

GENERAL MITCHELL'S BOMBERS SINK THE OSTFRIESLAND,
BY BOB LAVIN. One of the highlights of USAF history was ''Billy''
Mitchell's destruction by air bombardment of the captured
German battleship OSTFRIESLAND in July, 1921.

*New Records and Mitchell's Trial*

The decade of the twenties was notable for a series of record flights which demonstrated the advancing potential of the military airplane. Early in 1923, Major Henry H. Arnold directed the first in-flight refueling experiment, using two DeHavilland-4B aircraft interconnected by a hose. Later in the same year, Captain Lowell H. Smith and Lieutenant John P. Richter utilized this technique to set an endurance record of 37¼ hours.

The most outstanding flight of 1923 was made by Lieutenants Oakley G. Kelley and John A. Macready. Manning a Fokker T-2, they flew nonstop from New York to San Diego in 26 hours and 50 minutes, the first such transcontinental flight. The record lasted slightly more than a year. On June 23, 1924, Lieutenant Russell L. Maughan piloted a Curtiss PW-8 pursuit craft across the continent in less than 22 hours.

In the same year, the Air Service conducted the first round-the-world flight in history. On April 6, eight flyers in four specially build Douglas World Cruisers took off from Seattle, Washington. On September 28, after flying 26,345 miles in 175 days, two of the four planes returned triumphantly to Seattle.

Competing with planes and pilots of the Navy and foreign countries, the Air Service scored a great double victory in 1925. On October 12, Lieutenant Cy Bettis, flying a Curtiss R3C-2 racer, won the Pulitzer Trophy with an average speed of 249 miles an hour. Two weeks later, Lieutenant Jimmy Doolittle used the same plane, equipped with pontoons, to set a new seaplane record of 245.7 miles per hour, winning the Schneider Cup Race.

In the years since the *Ostfriesland* sinking, Billy Mitchell had continued his public blasts against Army and Navy authorities, still seeking greater status for the Air Service. In April, 1925, when his term as Assistant Chief of the Air Service expired, Mitchell was reduced to his permanent grade of lieutenant colonel and assigned a low level job in Texas. The climactic event of Mitchell's stormy career was triggered by the loss of the Navy dirigible *Shenandoah* in severe weather over Ohio, September, 1925. Mitchell felt that this and other disasters had been caused by ''the incompetency, criminal negligence and almost treasonable administration of the national defense by the Navy and War Departments.'' President Calvin Coolidge acted immediately and, along with Secretary of War John W. Weeks, preferred court martial charges. On December 17, ironically the anniversary of the first powered flight, Mitchell was found guilty and suspended from active duty for a period of five years. Soon after the verdict, Billy Mitchell resigned from the Air Service to continue his fight for air power as a civilian.

THE FIRST TRANSCONTINENTAL NON-STOP FLIGHT, BY HERB MOTT.
The flight was made on May 2–3, 1923, by Lieutenants Oakley G. Kelley and
John A. Macready.

## The Air Corps Is Born

The Air Service's assault on speed, altitude and endurance records continued. A notable achievement of 1926 was a new altitude mark set by the same Lieutenant John Macready who had participated in the first transcontinental nonstop flight; on January 29, Macready climbed to 38,704 feet.

Meanwhile, Billy Mitchell's campaign for greater exploitation of air power was beginning to show results. Late in 1925, the Lampert Committee of the House of Representatives recommended a *unified air force* independent of the Army and the Navy. At nearly the same time, the Morrow Board, appointed by President Coolidge to resolve the controversy created by Mitchell, rejected the idea of a *separate air arm* but proposed that the Air Service be given greater status and representation on the general staff.

On July 2, 1926, Congress acted upon the reports and passed legislation which created an Air Corps of the Army, ''thereby strengthening the conception of military aviation as an offensive striking arm rather than an auxiliary service.'' The act also created the position of Assistant Secretary of War for Air. Named to the post was F. Trubee Davison, who held it until 1932. Major General Mason Patrick was designated first Chief of the Air Corps.

The most important part of the act was provision of authority for a major five-year expansion. The new Air Corps had only 60 pursuit and 169 observation planes and a total inventory of fewer than 1,000 aircraft. Similarly, personnel strength had never come close to the 1920 authorization because of funding limitations. The expansion provided for a force of 1,800 modern aircraft manned by 1,650 officers and 15,000 enlisted men.

Late in the year the Air Corps decided to end experiments with its major lighter-than-air craft, the RS-1. Since 1920, the young air force had sought to develop airships with the eventual goal of using them as aircraft carriers. There had been a crushing set back in 1922, when the Air Service's 410-foot semirigid *Roma* crashed and burned at Norfolk, Virginia, killing 34. In 1925, the Army had started flying the Goodyear-built RS-1, a helium-inflated ship with a capacity of 710,000 cubic feet. Although the RS-1 was the largest semirigid built, its payload was insufficient for operational use and it was abandoned.

LIEUTENANT MACREADY (LEFT) BEFORE HIS RECORD HIGH ALTITUDE FLIGHT, BY PAUL CALLE.

*The Goodwill Flight and the Question Mark*

Led by Major Herbert A. Dargue, five Air Corps Loening COA-1 amphibians took off from Kelly Field, Texas, on December 21, 1926, on the first leg of a memorable flight of the twenties: a good will mission through Central and South America. The 10 flyers included several who were to become prominent in the Air Force of the future, among them Captain Ira C. Eaker, Lieutenant Ennis C. Whitehead and Lieutenant Muir S. Fairchild.

The 22,000-mile trip, which was to take almost five months, was marked by tragedy. Over Buenos Aires, a plane flown by Captain Clinton F. Woolsey and Lieutenant John W. Benton collided with the Dargue-Whitehead flagship. Dargue and Whitehead parachuted to safety, but Woolsey and Benton were killed. The remaining four planes completed the trip on May 2, 1927, at Bolling Field, Washington, D.C., where President Coolidge presented a Distinguished Flying Cross to each of the eight survivors.

Another notable flight took place on June 28-29, 1927. In a demonstration of the Air Corps' ability to navigate long distances over water, Lieutenants Lester J. Maitland and Albert F. Hegenberger flew a trimotor Fokker named *Bird of Paradise* from Oakland, California to Wheeler Field at Honolulu. They completed the 2,418-mile trip in 25 hours and 50 minutes.

The Fokker trimotor played another important part in Air Force history in 1929, when Air Corps flyers kept it aloft by means of the mid-air refueling technique for almost a week. The Fokker, the *Question Mark*, was commanded by a future USAF Chief of Staff, then Major Carl A. Spaatz. Also in the crew of five were Captain Eaker and Lieutenant Elwood R. Quesada, both of whom were later to attain general officer rank. The flight started on New Year's Day from Los Angeles Airport. A second plane, piloted by Captain Ross C. Hoyt and Lieutenant Odas Moon, served as the tanker-supplier, transferring not only fuel but food, batteries and a variety of other supplies. The planes made 43 contacts, nine of them at night, and some 40 tons of material were transferred. On January 7, the *Question Mark*'s port engine quit and Spaatz was forced to land. The *Question Mark* had remained in the air for 150 hours, 40 minutes, 15 seconds and had covered 11,000 miles.

*THE AIR CORPS GOODWILL FLIGHT, 1926–27, BY NEIL BOYLE.*
*The DETROIT was ill-fated; a mid-air collision cost the lives of its two-man crew.*

*Advances in Planes and Personnel*

On June 20, 1930, the Air Corps dedicated its new ''West Point of the Air'' at Randolph Field, Texas. Randolph Field became the headquarters for the Air Corps Training Center, and, a year later, the site of the primary and basic flying schools; advanced training was conducted at Kelly Field, Texas.

The dedication of the center fulfilled a long-time dream of the Air Corps, vigorously promoted for several years by pioneer Frank P. Lahm, who had reached the rank of major general. Throughout most of the decade of the thirties, all primary/basic training was provided by Randolph.

The early thirties also brought a number of advances in military aircraft. Throughout the twenties, the predominant aircraft in service had been left-over World War I ''stick-and-wire'' biplanes like the DeHavilland-4B and the Curtiss JN-4D ''Jenny.'' These and other ancient aircraft were now replaced with newly designed ones.

The most important of the new planes, from the standpoint of the Air Corps' offensive capability, were three all-metal, monoplane bombers. The Boeing B-9, a mid-wing monoplane with retractable landing gear, made its appearance in 1931. Powered by two 600-horsepower engines, the B-9 had a top speed of 188 miles per hour. In the same year the Air Corps introduced to service the metal Curtiss A-8 attack bomber, with speed characteristics comparable to those of the B-9.

In 1932, a still more advanced plane entered service. A streamlined monoplane, the Martin B-10 had enclosed cockpits and could carry more than a ton of bombs. It had a top speed of well over 200 miles an hour and could operate at altitudes as high as 28,000 feet. Until the B-10, the pursuit plane had enjoyed a great speed advantage over bombers; now bomber could outspeed fighter.

The national depression delayed the Air Corps' five-year expansion program but fortunately a major portion had been completed before the economic slump. By mid-1932, the Air Corps had grown to 1,300 officers and more than 13,000 enlisted men. It had 45 airplane squadrons, two airship and two ballon squadrons. Strength was still not up to the 1926 authorization, but the Air Corps had come a long way in terms of personnel and equipment.

*FORMATION OVER KELLY FIELD, 1932, BY KEITH FERRIS.*

## The Airmail Venture

The advent of the B-10 made possible a spectacular air event of 1934, a mission to determine the practicability of rapid reinforcement of outlying possessions. Hap Arnold, then a lieutenant colonel, led a flight of 10 B-10's on an 8,300-mile round-trip from Washington, D.C. to Alaska in July and August. The 30-man team set up a base at Fairbanks, Alaska and photographed 20,000 square miles of the territory before starting the return trip. The first leg was a non-stop mass formation flight from Juneau to Seattle, the first such flight between Alaska and the United States.

The mission, pointing up the potential of long-range craft, sparked an Air Corps drive for still another task: coastal defense against seaborne attack. For this purpose, Air Corps leaders like Arnold, Foulois and Brigadier General Frank M. Andrews advocated development of a fleet of long-range bombardment and observation aircraft. These planes would be assembled into a General Headquarters Air Force, a central strike force operating directly under the general staff of the Army. Foulois, now a major general and Chief of the Air Corps, initiated plans for a large, high-speed, high-altitude bomber with a range of more than 2,000 miles. In early development during 1934-35, this plane emerged as the famed Boeing B-17 Flying Fortress.

Meanwhile, the Air Corps was suffering through the worst of all of its peacetime ventures. In February, 1934, Postmaster General James A. Farley had canceled the government's airmail contracts with commercial airlines and turned the job of flying the mail over to the Air Corps. But the air arm of 1934 was ill-equipped for the task. Despite the arrival of new planes like the B-10, most Air Corps equipment was still obsolete. The military flyers had little or no experience in scheduled transport operations and they had no adequate ground organization and navigation aids to back up the service. Bad weather throughout the few months of the service lent its hand. Within the first month, there were nine fatal crashes. In May, the Air Corps was relieved of the assignment. The tragic airmail episode had one beneficial effect: it focused public attention on the inadequacy of military aviation.

LIEUTENANT COLONEL ''HAP'' ARNOLD AND CREW, BY HERB
MOTT. Arnold led 10 bombers on a mass flight to Alaska in 1934.

## Successes and Setbacks

While the Air Corps was living through its disastrous airmail experience, a War Department board was again studying the status of military aviation. Headed by former Secretary of War Newton D. Baker, the board issued its report in July, 1934. Once again the idea of a unified defense department and a separate air force was rejected. The board summed up its regard for air power in a single sentence: "Independent air missions have little effect upon the issue of battle and none upon the outcome of war."

Paradoxically the Baker Board endorsed the proposals for a GHQ Air Force. The War Department acted upon the recommendation and created the GHQ Air Force as of March 1, 1935. General Andrews was named its commander, with headquarters at Langley Field, Virginia. His command consisted of three wings of tactical units located at Langley, Barksdale (Louisiana) and March (California) Fields. The Air Corps continued in being as the supply and training element of the air arm and, in 1935, Major General Oscar Westover succeeded Foulois as its chief.

The experimental version of the B-17 started its flight tests in July, 1935. In August it made an impressive demonstration of its potential, flying from the Boeing plant at Seattle to Dayton, Ohio, 2,100 air miles at an average speed of 232 miles per hour.

The twin success — the arrival of the first real long-range bomber and the approval of the GHQ Air Force concept—prompted enthusiasm for the future among air officers. It was short-lived. The War Department had accepted in principle the concept of long-range bombardment, but it was still guided by the national principle of arming for defense rather than offense. Further, there were limited funds available and there was as much need for modernizing ground force equipment as there was for new airplanes. So when Andrews and his chief of staff, Colonel Hugh J. Knerr, asked for funds to purchase 65 B-17's in 1936, they were grudgingly allowed 13. In the fiscal year 1938, Andrews issued a new request for 50 B-17's to equip two wings. It was denied; the War Department instructed the Air Corps to buy, instead, the twin-engine Douglas B-18, which was smaller and less expensive.

THE BERLINER-JOYCE P-16 OVER OAKLAND
BAY, 1934, BY ROBERT WATKINS.

*War on the Horizon*

Men like Andrews, Arnold, Foulois, Knerr and Westover continued to emphasize the desperate need for a long-range striking force, including planes even more advanced than the B-17, but to little avail. The 13 B-17's delivered in 1937 constituted the total long-range airplane force until 1939.

The plans for a long-range force suffered further blows in 1938. A joint Army-Navy agreement limited the Air Corps to flights of no more than 100 miles off shore and gave the Navy responsibility for operations in ''the air above the ocean.'' Secretary of War Harry H. Woodring ordered the Air Corps to confine its offensive aircraft to light, medium and attack bombers. In May, 1938, Major General Stanley D. Embick summed up the position of the General Staff: ''1. Our national policy contemplates preparation for defense, not aggression. 2. Defense of sea areas . . . is a function of the Navy. 3. . . . If the equipment to be provided for the Air Corps be that best adapted to carry out the specific functions assigned it under Joint Action, there would appear to be no need for a plane larger than the B-17.''

Andrews was unrelenting in his opposition to this attitude, and, like Mitchell, he became a thorn in the side of the General Staff. When his tour as GHQ Air Force commander expired on March 1, 1939, he was demoted to his permanent rank of colonel and assigned the same unimportant job to which Mitchell had been consigned in 1925. Andrews, however, was soon to be vindicated and promoted to higher posts.

With a European war now on the horizon and an Air Corps expansion directed by President Roosevelt under way, the Army was forced to take a second look at the restrictions it had placed on its air arm. The Corps was given a new mission: defense of the Caribbean and Latin American approaches to the United States. This, obviously, called for long-range aircraft and belated orders were placed.

When the war broke out in Europe, the Air Corps had 800 ''first-line'' aircraft, first-line in name only, because more than 700 of them were rapidly becoming obsolete. The German Luftwaffe had 4,100 far-superior planes. The real build-up of the wartime air force started with President Roosevelt's May, 1940, call for 50,000 airplanes a year. At the start of the fateful year 1941, the Air Corps was a rapidly expanding but far from combat-ready service.

# CHAPTER III

# The War Against Germany

*Expansion and War*

In June, 1941, an organization known as the Army Air Forces was created to direct the activities of the Air Corps and the Air Force Combat Command. The AAF's commander was Major General H. H. Arnold, who had assumed the office of Chief of the Air Corps in 1938, on the death of General Westover.

There had been a steady flow of American-built planes to friendly nations in Europe for several months. Because of the demands of war, these nations found it difficult to supply pilots to ferry the aircraft to Europe, so General Arnold proposed that his pilots take on this job. Thus it was that the Ferrying Command, under Colonel Robert Olds, was created and within six months, it flew 1,350 planes across the Atlantic.

The real expansion of the AAF was now under way. Successive plans had increased the authorized strength to 54, then to 84 groups. The training objective had climbed to 30,000 pilots a year. Most of the pilot training was assigned to the Gulf Coast Training Center, and at Randolph Field a new class of 400 started training every five weeks. To meet the demand for specialists, the technical schools at Chanute, Scott and Lowry Fields were expanded to the bursting point and the overflow was diverted into civilian schools.

By the 1st of December, 1941, the AAF had grown to 23,000 officers, 16,000 cadets, 275,000 enlisted men and 12,000 aircraft. There were eight air forces, four within the continental limits of the United States and one each in the Philippines, Hawaii, Alaska and the Caribbean.

Then came December 7—Pearl Harbor. More than 350 Japanese carrier-based aircraft struck successive blows at Navy ships in Pearl Harbor, at Ford Island and at Kaneohe, and against the Army's Hickam and Wheeler Fields.

Within a day, President Roosevelt had issued a declaration of war against Japan. Three days later, Germany and Italy, Japan's Axis partners, declared war on the United States.

The AAF immediately went into action, moving its aircraft to bases in England via the North Atlantic ferry route, or, in the case of shorter-range planes, by sea transport. By year-end, there were 882 AAF planes, mostly Boeing B-17's and Douglas C-47 transports, in England.

NIGHT WATCH ON ASCENSION ISLAND, BY JACK LEVINE.

*In Europe and Africa*

In February, 1942, General Arnold dispatched Brigadier General Ira C. Eaker to England. Assignment—to set up a bomber command headquarters and prepare for the arrival of what was to become the Eighth Air Force. The combat units started to arrive in the spring, and before summer, Major General Carl A. Spaatz landed in England and took command of the Eighth.

In the meantime, the first American unit to participate in combat in western Europe flew its initial mission. The 15th Bombardment Squadron had been training with the British Royal Air Force, flying the RAF's Douglas Bostons. Six 15th BS crews joined an RAF attack on German airfields in Holland on July 4, 1942. Two of the American-manned planes were downed by flak.

The RAF and the Eighth Air Force established a coordinated system whereby the AAF B-17's, flying unescorted by fighters when necessary, would handle daylight bombing and the RAF would conduct night missions.

AAF ''heavies'' took off on their first England-based raid on August 17. Colonel Frank A. Armstrong, Jr., commanding officer of the 97th Bombardment Group, led 12 of his B-17 crews in an attack on railroad yards at Rouen-Sotteville, France; General Eaker flew in one of the planes. Six other aircraft of the 97th flew a diversionary mission. The RAF provided a formation of Spitfires for fighter escort, and opposition over Rouen-Sotteville was negligible. No planes were lost and the mission was successful.

While the Eighth Air Force was still being readied for combat, another AAF unit went into action. The German Afrika Corps under General Erwin Rommel was driving across the Libyan desert and the British sought U.S. support for bombing his supply lines in North Africa and southern Europe. A detachment of Consolidated B-24's, en route through Africa to China, was detoured to Egypt. Commanded by Colonel Harry Halvorsen, 12 B-24 crews flew a long-range mission against the vital oil refineries at Ploesti, Rumania, on June 12, 1942. The mission inflicted little damage, but no planes were lost to flak or enemy fighters; four planes, however, were forced to land in Turkey and their crews were interned.

AMERICAN EAGLES IN DISPERSAL HUT, BY FRANK BERESFORD.

*Preparations for Torch*

After its initial success at Rouen-Sotteville, the Eighth Air Force continued operations on a limited basis during summer and early fall of 1942. Formations were small and the targets were only a few hundred miles from the Eighth's bases in England. Bombing results were generally good, and on its first 11 missions the Eighth lost only two B-17's.

A major effort of 1942 took place on October 9, when the Eighth dispatched 108 heavies in an attack on the German stronghold at Lille, France. This time the AAF encountered heavy fighter opposition and four of the bombers were shot down. The remainder, under constant attack from German aircraft, managed to inflict some damage on Lille, but the mission was generally disappointing.

Meanwhile, the AAF had moved to strengthen its forces in the Middle East. In June, 1942, Major General Lewis H. Brereton brought a flight of nine B-17 Flying Fortresses from India to Cairo and set up the Middle East Air Force. The MEAF was strengthened in August by the addition of the 98th Bombardment Group (Heavy), the 12th Bombardment Group (Medium) and the 57th Fighter Group. The medium bombers and the fighters joined the RAF's Desert Air Force, supporting General Bernard L. Montgomery's Eighth Army in the great North African battle against Rommel's Afrika Corps. The heavy bombers, operating from Egypt, struck at the Desert Fox's supply lines. In November, the MEAF became the Ninth Air Force.

At this time, Allied forces were preparing for Operation Torch—the invasion of North Africa-to drive out Axis forces and, at the same time, prepare for the invasion of Italy from occupied African bases. For this operation, Lieutenant General Dwight D. Eisenhower was appointed commander of Allied Force Headquarters in London. To support the invasion, the AAF created a new air force, the Twelfth, under Brigadier General Jimmy Doolittle, with Colonel Hoyt S. Vandenberg as Chief of Staff. A large part of the strength of the Eighth Air Force was assigned to the Twelfth. The Eighth continued to operate from England during the winter, but on a limited basis. North Africa was, for the moment, Target One.

*FELLOW WORKERS, BY FRANK BERESFORD. The painting expresses the close teamwork that existed between the Army Air Forces and the Royal Air Force.*

*The AAF in Torch*

Torch was launched on November 8, 1942. In this first great amphibious operation of the war, three separate task forces under General Eisenhower attacked German, Italian and Vichy French forces along a wide front stretching from western Morocco to Algeria. In western North Africa, the French offered little resistance, and within three days Allied forces had taken Algiers, Oran, and Casablanca. The Allied armies drove eastward toward Tunisia, wedging the Axis forces between the invasion army on one side and General Montgomery's already positioned Eighth Army in the south of Tunisia.

In February, 1943, a desperate Axis counterattack temporarily stalled the Allied drive from the west, but Montgomery continued to move up from the south, and on April 7 the Eighth Army made contact with the invasion force. This contact formed an Allied ring around Axis troops located in a small corner of Tunisia.

The Allies started a final drive on May 4, and within three days American and British troops were able to occupy Bizerte and Tunis, the last Axis strongholds. On May 13 the Axis forces surrendered, leaving no Germans or Italians under arms in all of Africa.

Twelfth Air Force participation in the initial phase of Torch was light; it was largely confined to fighter support of the landings. After ground was secured by the invasion troops, the Twelfth moved into Africa and set up bases. Within a few days after the landings, the Twelfth's B-17's started strategic bombing of the Axis concentrations in Bizerte and Tunis.

As the Allied forces moved eastward toward Tunisia, the Twelfth's fighters and medium bombers supported the movement, striking at Axis troops and shipping in the Mediterranean, while the heavy bombers continued to pound Tunisian targets with increasing frequency and in increasing numbers. In February, 1943, the British and American air units in northwest Africa were merged into the Northwest African Air Forces under General Spaatz.

Prior to the final drive in May, the NAAF's B-17's were given new assignments: blasting Axis reinforcement convoys in the Mediterranean and destroying the ports in Italy, Sicily and Sardinia which might have been used for evacuation of Axis troops from Tunisia. In the last weeks of the war in Africa, the NAAF and the Ninth Air Force supporting Montgomery combined in a devastating series of attacks on Tunisia and the Mediterranean area which contributed in great measure to the swift conclusion of Torch.

GROUND CREW AT WORK IN NORTH AFRICA, BY MILTON MARX.

*Sicily and Italy*

The next objective of the Allied advance was Sicily, the island off the toe of Italy's boot, occupation of which would open the Mediterranean to Allied convoys. A necessary preliminary involved taking the smaller island of Pantelleria, midway between the northeastern tip of Tunisia and Sicily.

For a solid month after the Axis surrender in Tunisia, NAAF planes pounded Pantelleria, flying more than 5,000 sorties and dropping some 6,200 tons of bombs on the island. On June 11, 1943, before assault forces could reach Pantelleria, the garrison commander ran up a white flag. Air power alone had won an important battle.

Now the Northwest African Air Forces turned attention toward Sicily. NAAF planes bombed Sicilian bases, sought out the enemy in the skies above the Mediterranean and all but eliminated air opposition. Then they struck at bases in Italy and France from which the Axis might fly defensive missions against the invasion. On July 10, the American Seventh and British Eighth Armies landed in Sicily, supported by almost 1,100 NAAF air sorties. Sicily was secured on August 18. In the meantime, impending defeat had caused the post-Mussolini Italian government to sue for armistice.

On September 8 and 9, Allied forces moved into Italy and advanced northward. Within a month, the American Fifth Army took Naples and the British Eighth secured the Foggia area, where the Axis had built a number of large air bases. This provided a complex from which the AAF's strategic bombers could hammer at targets in central and eastern Europe.

For this purpose, the AAF created a new air force, the Fifteenth, with headquarters in Bari, Italy, and its heavy bombardment units concentrated in the Foggia-Cerignola area. Nucleus of the Fifteenth was the heavy bomber complement of the Twelfth Air Force, bolstered by new groups from the United States. Major General Nathan F. Twining was named as the Fifteenth's commander.

The Fifteenth was formed on November 1, 1943 and it flew its initial mission on the following day. The target complex was a group of aircraft and parts plants at Wiener-Neustadt, Austria. The raid was an extremely effective one, reducing the complex to minimal production for a period of four months. The Fifteenth followed up with daily raids against airfields and industrial targets in Germany, Italy and the Balkans in a program designed to cripple enemy fighter production.

*MEDIUMS OVER LEGHORN, BY JOHN LAVALLE.*

*Ploesti and Regensburg/Schweinfurt*

While Allied forces were eliminating Axis opposition in Africa, two of the greatest strategic bombing missions of the war were conducted, one from Africa and one from England.

The first was the low-level attack on Ploesti on August 1, 1943. Ploesti was a vital target. Its refineries were producing one third of all the oil available to the Axis. Located in the southeast corner of Rumania, it was beyond the range of the England-based bombers of the Eighth Air Force. It was, however, possible to reach the target from bases in Libya held by the British. For the attack, the Ninth Air Force assembled five groups of B-24's and planned a minimum altitude crossing of southeastern Europe in an effort to achieve surprise.

However, the low altitude made navigation extremely difficult and the first planes inadvertently flew close to Bucharest, south of Ploesti, alerting enemy defenses. Flak and fighter opposition was intense and 54 of the 177 B-24's which took off from Bengasi failed to return. However, the mission knocked out 40 percent of Ploesti's cracking and refining capacity.

Two weeks later, the Eighth Air Force challenged German fighter defenses in an unescorted dual mission deep into Germany, the targets being the Messerschmitt production plants at Regensburg and the ball-bearing works at Schweinfurt, manufacturing complexes necessary to Germany's fighter production. The plan called for one large formation to hit Regensburg and avoid German defenses on the return trip by flying south to Algeria, now in American hands. A second formation would follow shortly thereafter to attack Schweinfurt, hopefully free of fighter attack because the German Luftwaffe would have committed its forces to the Regensburg battle.

On August 17, 146 B-17's of the Eighth Air Force struck at Regensburg without fighter escort beyond the Belgian border. For an hour and a half they were under constant fighter attack, losing 24 planes but reaching the target and inflicting heavy damage. They escaped to the south without further loss. The Schweinfurt mission was delayed more than three hours by weather, giving the Luftwaffe time to refuel and re-attack. The Eighth made 80 direct hits on the ball-bearing plants, but it was a costly effort; 36 of the 230 bombers were shot down.

OVER THE ALPS ON THE REGENSBURG RAID, BY FRANK BERESFORD.

*Another Schweinfurt; A Reassessment*

If the first Schweinfurt raid was a tragedy, the second, on October 14, 1943, was a disaster. This time the Eighth mounted an attack of 291 B-17's, again escorted only as far as the German border. The Luftwaffe introduced a new menace to strategic bombing: the rocket-firing fighter.

German tactics consisted of teaming the twin-engine rocket-equipped planes with fast and maneuverable ME109's and other single-engine fighters. After the initial attack by the latter, the rocket launchers would lob their deadly missiles into a B-17 formation, causing the formation to spread and breaking down the bombers' concentration of firepower. Then the single-engine fighters would strike again, at the stragglers. All the way through Germany and back to the border, the Eighth Air Force Fortresses were under constant attack, but they somehow managed an accurate, destructive drop on the already crippled Schweinfurt industrial complex. The Forts shot down 35 German fighters, but it was a hollow victory; on that single mission, 60 of the bombers, almost one out of every five, went down.

General Arnold and his top commanders were forced to reassess their views on unescorted strategic bombing. The bombers had injured Germany's industrial capacity, but not enough to justify the heavy losses sustained by the Eighth Air Force. The fighters in Europe did not have the range to provide escort deep into Germany. Belatedly, long-range escort versions of the Republic P-47, Lockheed P-38 and North American P-51 were being built in the United States. Until they became available for combat, the Eighth had to confine its bombing to targets closer to home base, where the shorter-range fighters could provide some protection.

At year-end, a new organization called United States Strategic Air Forces in Europe was set up to coordinate the activities of the Eighth in England and the Fifteenth in Italy. General Spaatz was assigned its command and General Doolittle took over the Eighth.

At the same time, the first long-range escort fighters began arriving in Europe. In its first month of operations with the P-51, the 4th Fighter Group scored 156 kills during escort missions. Now the Eighth was able to resume its attack on the industrial heart of Germany. The top planners were preparing for an invasion of the continent and a necessary prelude was the achievement of air superiority; that required destruction of the Luftwaffe in the air, on the ground and on the production lines.

*RETREAT AT ELVEDEN HALL, BY FRANK BERESFORD.*

*The Fight for Air Superiority*

By early 1944, the Eighth Air Force had grown into a massive organization. The long-range, high-performance fighters were arriving by the hundreds and the bombardment force was strengthened by a steady flow of new planes and crews.

Now Doolittle was able to mount really large-scale missions which, at times, saw more than 1,000 bombers carrying their payloads of destruction into the German homeland. In a single week in February, 1944, the Eighth blasted German aircraft manufacturing facilities with 3,300 sorties.

In March, the Eighth carried the war to Berlin, escorted all the way by the P-51's German pilots had learned to respect. On March 4, 6 and 8, Berlin was hammered by 1,000-plane raids. It was the beginning of the end for the German air war machine.

The fighters were no longer interested in just protecting their bombers. They flew far in advance of the formations, seeking out the Luftwaffe and outfighting it. In February and March the Germans lost some 800 fighters in the west alone, and the bombing raids were delivering telling blows to the German industry's ability to replace the lost planes.

Germany had, meanwhile, attempted to counter the raids by dispersing its manufacturing industry, breaking it down into small, widely scattered plants, many of them underground. But it was too late; 75 percent of the fighter plane production capacity had been destroyed. The fierce air battles over Germany had claimed the cream of the Luftwaffe's skilled pilots. Reduced in numbers of planes and in the skill level of their operators, the Luftwaffe lost effectiveness day by day.

It was perhaps the most notable contribution of the war for air power. The advocates of strategic bombing had been vindicated. Fighters and bombers working in concert had gained air superiority, the requisite for the advance of ground forces onto the continent. The stage was set for Overlord—the invasion.

*HANGAR QUEEN, BY PETER HURD. Every squadron had its
"hangar queen," the gremlin-plagued plane that was more
frequently out of service for maintenance than it was operational.*

*A Second Air Front*

The Fifteenth and Twelfth Air Forces had also played major roles in breaking the back of the Luftwaffe.

Late in 1943, the Allies had organized the Mediterranean Allied Air Force, an amalgamation of all AAF and RAF units in the theater. In January, 1944, Lieutenant General Ira C. Eaker, who had headed the Eighth Air Force for the previous year, arrived in Italy to take command of the MAAF. General Eaker's Director of Operations was an airman destined to become a top leader of the post-war Air Force: Brigadier General Lauris C. Norstad.

The MAAF was subdivided into two major components: the Mediterranean Allied Tactical Air Force and the Mediterranean Allied Strategic Air Force. The Twelfth Air Force was the American element of the tactical organization, the Fifteenth the United States' portion of MASAF. General Twining continued to head the Fifteenth and Major General John K. Cannon commanded the Twelfth.

The Mediterranean theater had become of secondary importance as far as ground operations were concerned, but it was of particular importance as a "second air front." In January and February, 1944, the Fifteenth teamed with the Eighth in the strategic air war, striking at targets in Italy, Austria, Germany and at the oil supplies in Rumania.

In mid-March, MAAF commenced a new type of air operation, an effort designed to kill German resistance in Italy by cutting off the flow of supplies from the north. Operation Strangle, it was called, and appropriately so. MAAF's fighter-bombers smashed bridges and crippled the Italian railway system. The mediums and heavies attacked railroad marshalling yards and shipping. In less than two months, MAAF flew more than 50,000 sorties in Strangle. By mid-May the Italian railroad network was a mass of twisted steel and rail traffic had all but ceased. Such supplies as the Germans were able to move to their troops at the front had to be brought in by truck and at night. This system obviously could not supply the 15 German divisions remaining in Italy. The enemy defenses in Italy had truly been "Strangled."

LIEUTENANT GENERAL
IRA C. EAKER,
BY NICOLAI FECHIN.

*The Tactical Air War in Italy*

On May 11, 1944, Allied ground forces in Italy started a major offensive, kicking off with a new drive against the German stronghold at Cassino, which had three times earlier resisted attack. Cassino was one of the most heavily defended points in the German Gustav Line, which stretched across Italy from Gaeta, north of Naples, to Pescara on the Adriatic Sea.

This time the Polish Corps and elements of the Eighth Army succeeded in blasting through the line, occupying the Abbey of Monte Cassino. From that start, the whole Allied front surged northward in Italy. The Germans abandoned the Gustav line and fell back to a new line far to the north. In the retreat, they declared Rome an open city, and on June 4 troops of the American Fifth Army entered it.

The Allies continued to press forward taking, in rapid succession, Pescara, Arezzo, Ancona, Leghorn and Florence. The Germans dug in at a new "Gothic Line" just north of Leghorn, Florence and Ancona, temporarily stalling the Allied advance.

Throughout this campaign, MAAF's tactical units continued to slash the enemy supply lines and to provide air support for the advancing ground armies. In June, MAAF's 280 combat squadrons flew more than 50,000 sorties, earning the respect of the ground troops for their well-coordinated direct support missions.

MAAF squadrons also unveiled a new technique for further confounding the disorderly German retreat. Working to the north of a retreating column, they would create a roadblock by bombing out a portion of the road. As traffic backed up with nowhere to go, fighter-bombers would attack the trapped column. In six weeks this technique accounted for the destruction of an estimated 5,000 German surface vehicles and heavy troop casualties.

The AAF had proved its worth on two European fronts and in the battle for Africa. Now it was to join sea and surfaces forces in the greatest of all battles—Overlord.

*THE LIGHTNINGS FORM UP, BY JOHN LAVALLE. The canvas depicts the start of a mission, over a base in Italy in 1944.*

*D-Day at Normandy*

In addition to the strategic air war being waged by General Spaatz' USSTAF, pre-invasion preparations involved large-scale tactical air operations along the French Channel coast and more than a hundred miles inland. This assignment fell to the AAF's Ninth Air Force and the British 2d Tactical Air Force.

General Brereton and his fighter commander, Brigadier General Elwood R. Quesada, had brought the nucleus of the Ninth to England from the Mediterranean in October, 1943. In England, the Ninth was reorganized and resupplied with large numbers of medium bombers, fighter bombers and troop carrier aricraft, becoming the world's largest tactical air force.

As a prelude to Overlord, in the early months of 1944, the Ninth was given a multiple assignment: destruction of roads, bridges and railways to block movement of German reserve units to the D-Day assault area; destruction of the Luftwaffe's airdromes near the planned beachheads to prevent air reinforcement; and destruction of Germany's coastal defenses.

A prime target of the Ninth's mediums and fighter bombers, together with planes of the 2d TAF and the Eighth Air Force, was the French railway system. In a large-scale pre-invasion campaign, Allied bombers dropped 76,000 tons of bombs on tracks, bridges and marshalling yards and all but eliminated rail movement in the area. The Ninth and 2d TAF also pounded Channel coast installations, including radar warning stations and V-1 ''buzz bomb'' bases, and dropped 6,700 tons of bombs on German airfields within 130 miles of the assault area

D-Day—the Sixth of June, 1944—the Allies landed on the continent. The Eighth and Ninth Air Forces and the RAF blackened the sky over Normandy with 171 squadrons of support aircraft, while the Twelfth and Fifteenth flew diversionary missions from Italy in an attempt to dilute what fighter defenses the Germans could muster. The IX Troop Carrier Command and the RAF dropped three airborne divisions on the Cherbourg peninsula. The Eighth and Ninth Air Forces flew more than 8,700 combat sorties on D-Day. There was practically no German air resistance in the beachhead area; the Allied air forces had contributed immeasurably to the success of the landings in their months of attack on the Luftwaffe.

As the beachheads were secured and Allied troops moved inland, the Ninth Air Force flew thousands of sorties on highly effective close support missions. An unsung group which made an enormous contribution was the IX Engineer Command, which moved in with the assault troops and built an emergency landing field in Normandy on D-Day. Working at times under fire, the engineers quickly hewed out a number of operational fields, and only a week after D-Day, fighter-bombers were operating from Normandy.

AMERICAN PLANES OVER THE ENGLISH COUNTRYSIDE, BY HARRISON STANDLEY.

*Invasion in the South*

The Eighth Air Force, now working most of the time as a tactical force, and the Ninth provided another great assist to the ground advance on July 25, 1944. About 1,500 heavies of the Eighth and 900 mediums and fighter-bombers of the Ninth conducted a massive saturation bombing along five miles of German defenses near Saint-Lo. It was an extremely effective raid, opening a hole in the enemy line through which Lieutenant General George S. Patton was able to move his Third Army. Patton drove across Normandy and into Brittany, supported by fighter-bombers of the XIX Tactical Air Command.

As ground forces swept across France, the Ninth—now commanded by Major General Hoyt S. Vandenberg—moved with them, shifting its bases from the beachhead area deeper into France and eastern Belgium.

Now the Allies attempted to drive quickly into Germany. On September 17, the AAF mounted an airborne operation designed to capture a 65-mile area of the Netherlands from which Montgomery's British troops might be able to outflank German defenses and slip into North Germany. The initial air drops were highly successful, but bad weather delayed airborne reinforcements and the Germans were able to stall the offensive.

In the meantime, Allied troops had secured new land on the continent. American and French forces from bases in the Mediterranean had landed on the French Riviera, the operation very effectively supported by General Eaker's MAAF. As prelude to the landings, the Fifteenth Air Force dropped heavy bomb tonnage on German defenses in southern France. During the assault, MAAF troop carriers delivered some 5,000 paratroops and the Twelfth Air Force provided beachhead cover and close support.

The southern invasion force occupied Marseilles, then moved rapidly up the Rhone valley, the Twelfth continuing to provide precision support. In a little more than three weeks, the Allies were able to free more than half of France, and on September 11 they met with Eisenhower's western invasion force.

66

BOMBS AWAY, BY JOHN LAVALLE

### The Battle of the Bulge

Adolf Hitler and his generals spent November and part of December, 1944, collecting what reserve strength was available for a counter-offensive against the advancing Allied armies. The intent of this countermove was to strike through Belgium's Ardennes Forest to retake Antwerp and split the Allied forces.

On December 16, the Germans launched the attack and some Panzer units were able to move as far as 50 miles through the thinly spread American lines before they were halted. This created a bulge in Allied lines and gave the name to one of the greatest actions of the war—the Battle of the Bulge.

The most fiercely contested engagement of the Bulge took place at Bastogne, where German panzers surrounded the 101st Airborne Division and made an all-out attack on the town. For a week the Germans were aided by bad weather that precluded air support for the 101st, but Bastogne held. On December 23 the weather cleared and waves of cargo planes were able to resupply the troops at Bastogne. Medium bombers of the Ninth Air Force blasted the railroads leading into the Ardennes, the Eighth struck at marshalling yards further back, and fighter-bombers of the Ninth strafed and bombed enemy columns in the hills of Belgium. For five straight days, the Ninth flew an average of 1,400 sorties a day against the Bulge.

American reinforcements broke through to Bastogne and the Germans, their supplies hit hard by the air strikes, started a withdrawal on January 8, 1945.

Meanwhile, the depleted Luftwaffe was making a last-gasp effort. Somehow the Germans had managed to scrape together enough air strength to provide good support to the Bulge attack, but on December 24, 1,400 heavy bombers of the Eighth hammered the 11 German airfields in the area and wiped out half of the Luftwaffe's Bulge aircraft.

On New Year's Day, the Luftwaffe retaliated with what was to prove its last major offensive. Some 800 planes attacked Allied airdromes in Belgium and the Netherlands. They scored heavy damage, putting 260 Allied aircraft out of commission, but in the process the Luftwaffe lost 200 of its own planes. It was a heavy price to pay, for, while the aircraft manufacturing arsenal in the United States was turning out thousands of planes a month, Germany's industry was all but wiped out.

*AIR EVACUATION BY L-5, BY JOHN SCOTT*

## The Thrust to the Elbe

After the Bulge. Allied armies moved rapidly eastward to the Rhine River, then across it into the once-rich German industrial area, the Ruhr. On April 1, the United States First and Ninth Armies completed encirclement of the Ruhr and soon more than 300,000 German troops defending the area capitulated. Swiftly, Allied forces moved on a broad front through Germany toward the Elbe River. On April 25, American and Soviet troops made contact at Torgau, a city on the Elbe about 100 miles south of Berlin.

Throughout this advance, the Allied tactical air forces were extremely active. The medium bombers raided enemy oil and ammunition supplies and struck at targets like rail and road bridges, marshalling yards and communications objectives. The fighters supplied close air support for the ground drive, escorted the medium bombers, flew reconnaissance missions and conducted counter-air operations against the remnants of the Luftwaffe, which was rarely able to offer more than token resistance.

The USSTAF heavies were less active. As more and more of Germany was occupied, they had fewer and fewer targets, although they did operate as tactical forces in the drive to the Elbe. On April 14 and 16, USSTAF heavies flew 1,200-plane raids against a pocket of German resistance near Bordeaux, saturating the area with demolition, incendiary and napalm bombs. These were very effective strikes which helped French ground forces take the region shortly thereafter.

The last strategic bombing of an industrial target took place on April 25, when the Eighth Air Force dropped 500 tons of bombs on the Skoda works at Pilsen, Czechoslovakia. From that point on, the Eighth had no more combat assignments. It was used, however, on mercy missions, dropping tons of food to the starving population of the Netherlands and evacuating prisoners of war liberated from camps in Germany.

On May 7, Germany surrendered. It was a fitting commentary on air power's contribution to the defeat of the Reich that General Spaatz and a number of other air officers were invited to participate in the surrender ceremonies at Reims on that day and at Berlin on May 9, 1945.

*EARLY EVENING IN THE DISPERSAL AREA, BY HARRISON STANDLEY.*

*Victory and Air Power*

In the course of the war against Germany, AAF strength had reached a peak of more than 13,000 combat planes operated by a force of 619,000 officers and men assigned to combat commands. Planes of the AAF flew more than 750,000 bombardment missions and about 1,000,000 fighter sorties, dropping nearly 1,500,000 tons of bombs and destroying some 35,000 enemy aircraft.

Statistics, however, cannot measure the true effectiveness of the AAF. Its real contribution lies in the extent that its might and prowess furthered the destruction of Germany's military strength and resources. There can be no doubt that air power played an important part in the defeat of Hitler's Reich, although the degree of contribution has been and will probably continue to be a matter of controversy.

To find out just how effective air power had been, President Roosevelt established, in September, 1944, the United States Strategic Bombing Survey, headed by insurance executive Franklin D'Olier. In its postwar report, the Survey made a summary statement which serves as a monument to the efforts of all Allied airmen in the European war:

"Allied air power was decisive in the war in western Europe. Hindsight inevitably suggests that it might have been employed differently or better in some respects. Nevertheless, it was decisive. In the air, its victory was complete; at sea, its contribution, combined with naval power, brought an end to the enemy's greatest naval threat—the U-boat; on land, it helped turn the tide overwhelmingly in favor of Allied ground forces. Its power and superiority made possible the success of the invasion. It brought the economy which sustained the enemy's armed forces to virtual collapse, although the full effects of this collapse had not reached the enemy's front lines when they were overrun by Allied forces. It brought home to the German people the full impact of modern war with all its horror and suffering. Its imprint on the German nation will be lasting."

TECHNICAL SERGEANT FOR-
REST L. VOSLER, BY CHARLES
BASKERVILLE. Sergeant Vosler
was an AAF Medal of Honor
winner.

FOUR ACES, BY CHARLES BASKERVILLE. Among the top
heroes of the war in Europe were these aces: foreground,
Colonel Hubert Zemke; center, Lieutenant Colonel Francis
Gabreski; lower right, Captain Robert S. Johnson; upper right,
Major Walker Mahurin.

LIEUTENANT WILLIAM BENEDICT AND P-40, BY CHARLES
BASKERVILLE. Lieutenant Benedict, an ace flying from Italy,
typifies the AAF fighter pilot.

# CHAPTER IV

# The War Against Japan

*Pearl Harbor and the Philippines*

When the Japanese attacked Hickam Field at 0755, December 7, 1941, the Army Air Forces had 231 planes at bases in the Islands. By nightfall, 64 of them had been completely destroyed and only 79 aircraft remained in commission.

Despite the surprise of the attack, the AAF managed to get some of its planes in the air. Some 48 sorties were flown in a futile search for the enemy's carriers while fighter units vainly attempted to stop the bombardment. The most successful effort came from the 47th Pursuit Squadron, whose field at Haleiwa had escaped damage. Six pilots in Curtiss P-40 and P-36 fighters intercepted the Japanese second wave. One of them, Lieutenant George S. Welch, claimed four Japanese aircraft. In all, however, the Japanese lost only 29 of the several hundred attacking planes.

A few hours later, another Japanese force launched an air and sea attack against the Philippines, where the Far East Air Force had 33 B-17's and 90 fighters.

FEAF, under General Brereton, had been forewarned of the attack and was able to put most of its aircraft into the air, but many were damaged or destroyed as they landed for refueling, and additional numbers were shot down in the air battle. Eighteen of the B-17's were lost, and the pursuit fleet was similarly cut down.

The AAF countered with its first offensive operation—an attack against a Japanese convoy steaming toward Luzon—on December 9 and 10. Five B-17's of the 14th Bombardment Squadron, led by Major Emmett O'Donnell, went after the Japanese ships in the South China Sea, scoring some hits. Piloting one of the B-17's was the AAF's first hero of the Pacific War, Captain Colin Kelly. He attacked a large warship (at first believed to be the battleship *Haruna*, but later identified as the heavy cruiser *Ashigara*) and his bombardier, Sergeant Meyer Levin, dropped the load of three 600-pound bombs and apparently scored one hit, setting the ship afire. Enemy fighters, however, shot down the B-17. Most of the crew jumped to safety but Kelly and Technical Sergeant William J. Delehanty were killed in the action.

*BOMBING OF THE ASHIGARA, BY PETER HURD. Captain Colin Kelly became the AAF's first hero of the Pacific war with his attack on the Japanese heavy cruiser ASHIGARA in the South China Sea.*

## The Doolittle Raid

In the next several months the Japanese swept through the Pacific against little or no opposition. They conquered the Philippines, Singapore and Malaya, Guam and Wake and moved into the Netherlands East Indies, securing footholds in New Guinea, New Britain and the Solomon Islands. In the North Pacific, they landed troops on Kiska and Attu in the Aleutian Islands. On the Asian land mass, they took most of Burma and isolated China.

In the midst of these continuing Japanese victories, the AAF launched a mission that was to become a legend and delivered an amazing blow against Japan itself. On April 1, 1942, 16 North American B-25 medium bombers of the 17th Bombardment Group were loaded aboard the aircraft carrier *Hornet* at Alameda, California, for what was to be the most daring air mission of the war. Leader of the 16 crews was Jimmy Doolittle, at that time a lieutenant colonel. The plan was to bring the *Hornet*, protected by Navy Task Force 16, into position 400 miles east of Tokyo and to send the bombers from the tiny carrier deck on a strike against the heart of the enemy.

On April 18 the task force was still more than 800 miles off Japan, when the danger of an encounter with enemy ships forced a premature take-off. First up was Doolittle, who led his 16 planes on a low-level, surprise attack on Tokyo, smashing factories, docks, oil dumps and supply depots. A lucky, unpredicted tailwind made it possible for all the planes (except one which ended up in Vladivostok) to reach the China coast, where the crews bailed out. Doolittle made his way to Chungking, where he was picked up by an American transport. Eight of the Tokyo raiders were captured, three of them executed.

Meanwhile, Allied forces were regrouping in Australia and New Guinea. In April, General Douglas MacArthur assumed command of the Southwest Pacific Area. Under him, as commander of the Allied Air Forces, was Lieutenant General George H. Brett. Together with Admiral Chester W. Nimitz, commander of the Pacific Ocean Areas, MacArthur planned a counteroffensive. First target was to be Guadalcanal in the Solomons, where Japanese occupation posed a threat to the Allied supply line to Australia.

CHAPEL ON GUADALCANAL, BY ROBERT LAESSIG.

*Guadalcanal and New Guinea*

The campaign against the Solomons was primarily the responsibility of the fleet, but the AAF joined Navy and Marine pilots in the battle for air superiority over Guadalcanal. Victory in the air made possible an amphibious assault on the island, and on August 7 the First Marine Division secured a beachhead. Shortly thereafter the Marines captured the enemy airstrip which, as Henderson Field, was to provide a base for operations by planes of the AAF and the Marine Corps.

Victory at Guadalcanal was assured in November, 1942, although pockets of Japanese resistance held out until February, 1943. The Japanese sent a convoy to reinforce the island garrison, but American ships and planes wiped out all 11 transports carrying more than 13,000 Japanese troops.

In the meantime, there was an intense battle for jointly-occupied New Guinea and allied air units were engaged in a bitter fight for control of the air. Major General George C. Kenney had taken over the Allied Air Forces in the area, and in September, 1942, he organized the Fifth Air Force from United States units in Australia and New Guinea. Kenney set up headquarters in Brisbane, Australia and a combat headquarters, under Brigadier General Ennis C. Whitehead, in New Guinea.

Heavy and medium bombers of the Fifth worked over the Japanese airfields at Buna and Lae, the major enemy strongpoints in New Guinea, while the fighters—notably the Lockheed P-38's—sought control of the skies. By mid-September, the Fifth Air Force ''owned the air'' over New Guinea, and the Allied ground offensive got under way. On January 2, 1943, MacArthur's troops took Buna and moved toward Lae, supported by the Fifth Air Force.

In the Solomons, the Thirteenth Air Force, under Major General Nathan F. Twining, was blasting the Japanese forces still holding out on Guadalcanal. In February, Allied forces secured Guadalcanal and launched an attack on New Georgia Island. The Thirteenth provided air support and flew heavy bombardment and reconnaissance missions in what was to become an extended campaign.

HENDERSON FIELD, GUADALCANAL, BY ROBERT LAESSIG.

## Action in the Aleutians

While the Allied counteroffensive in the South Pacific was gaining momentum, the AAF was active in an effort to drive the Japanese out of the Aleutians. The AAF organization in this area was the Eleventh Air Force, headed by Major General William O. Butler.

Late in 1942, United States forces had taken the island of Adak without opposition and set up an air base. Early in 1943, a second base at Amchitka became available, and from these bases planes of the Eleventh conducted repeated strikes against the Japanese strongholds at Attu and Kiska. Operations were limited, however, by the worst weather experienced in any theater of war.

In April and May, 1943, reasonably good weather—it never became entirely good—permitted a step-up of the Eleventh's activity. In a short period in April, the Eleventh flew 1,175 sorties with an average of only 226 aircraft, softening up Attu and Kiska for planned invasions.

The Army and Navy jointly launched Operation Landgrab, the invasion of Attu, on May 11, with the Eleventh providing air support. Once again, weather hampered air operations and Japanese land forces offered stiff resistance. By the end of the month, however, Attu was secured.

The capture of this island gave the Eleventh a base from which even its medium bombers could strike at the northern islands of Japan, the Kuriles. The initial mission, the first attack on the Japanese homeland since Doolittle's raid, was made by eight B-25's on July 10. In succeeding months, the Eleventh continued to hit the Kuriles with both heavy and medium bombers.

The invasion of Kiska on August 15th, 1943, proved to be anticlimactic. Contrary to expectations, invading ground forces did not encounter a single Japanese soldier; the enemy had vanished. Continued pre-invasion pounding by AAF and Navy planes and a Navy surface task group had convinced the Japanese commander that evacuation was in order, and he was able to withdraw his garrison by sea under cover of fog.

CLEARING WEATHER IN THE ALEUTIANS, BY OGDEN PLEISSNER.

*The Capture of Munda*

In mid-1943, the battle for New Guinea was still raging and the Fifth Air Force was in the thick of it. After the fall of Buna, MacArthur's next objectives were Salamaua and Lae, to the west of Buna. Before attempting a ground advance on these strongholds, it was necessary to reduce enemy air strength at an air base complex in the vicinity of Wewak, 300 miles to the west of Lae.

In August, bombers of the Fifth Air Force made a mass raid on the Wewak complex and destroyed 175 Japanese planes, making a significant dent in Japan's air strength in New Guinea. Then, with the aid of a perfectly executed airborne drop, MacArthur's forces smashed Japanese resistance at Salamaua and Lae.

In the Solomons, Allied forces had driven the Japanese from the New Georgia island group. The capture of the airfield at Munda made available an important base, one from which the fighters, light and medium bombers of the Thirteenth Air Force could range throughout the Solomons. Engineers quickly repaired the battle damage and operations started on October 5. Before the year was out, Munda was the most heavily trafficked airfield in the South Pacific.

The stage was set for the final phase of the drive through the Solomons, the capture of Bougainville. Largest of the Solomons, with good harbors, many airfields and heavy defenses, Bougainville was a key objective of the two-pronged counteroffensive in New Guinea and the Solomons.

*MUNDA AIR BASE, NEW GEORGIA, BY ROBERT LAESSIG.*

*Clearing the Solomons*

For the pre-invasion bombardment of Bougainville, General Twining—now commander of all air forces in the Solomons—had two groups of B-24's based at Guadalcanal, 48 B-25's and 148 Navy and Marine Corps torpedo and dive bombers based at Munda. At Munda and other bases, he also had a strong force of fighters and miscellaneous aircraft; in all, a combat force of 650 planes, the largest yet assembled in the South Pacific.

Twining's air assault got under way on October 18, 1943. It was an intensive assault and a highly diversified one, as air commanders drew upon the capabilities of the many different types of aircraft which made up the Solomons air force. Focal points of the assault were the airfields of Bougainville and the heaviest raids were made by the AAF component of the mixed force.

On November 1, the ''AirSol'' force switched to invasion support as the Third Marine Division landed on Bougainville. The Japanese put up terrific resistance on the island, but they were slowly driven back and split into isolated groups during November and December. The AirSol force hammered at enemy shipping around the island and attacked land targets in advance of the Marine Corps drive. By mid-December, it was plain that the Japanese were through in the Solomons, although pockets of resistance remained.

United States forces initiated a new campaign on another front on November 13, a drive against the Gilbert and Marshall Islands in the Central Pacific. Here the AAF component was the Seventh Air Force, under Major General Willis Hale and later Major General Robert Douglass, Jr. Initially based in Hawaii and later in the Ellice Islands, the Seventh was assigned the primary task of bombing the islands of the Central Pacific to soften them up for invasion; ''One damned island after another'' was its unofficial motto. The Seventh flew hundreds of sorties against places like Tarawa, Makin, Wotje, Jaluit, Maloelap and Kwajalein. After the fall of Tarawa in November, 1943, the Seventh set up bases there for further strikes against Japanese positions in the Marshalls.

NIGHT FIGHTER OVER BOUGAINVILLE, BY
ROBERT LAESSIG. *The plane is the Northrop
P-61 Black Widow.*

*The Air Battle of New Britain*

While the Navy task force was landing on Bougainville, General Kenney's Fifth Air Force was paving the way for another advance northward. By this time, MacArthur's forces in New Guinea had advanced to Finschafen, a point on the northern coast of New Guinea directly opposite the Japanese stronghold of New Britain. The Fifth Air Force started a campaign to win air superiority over New Britain and New Ireland, northeast and very close to New Guinea. This was an air campaign of the first magnitude, because the two islands boasted enormous air, troop and sea strength. The key point of the attack was the town of Rabaul on the northern tip of New Britain. Intelligence credited Rabaul alone with 367 antiaircraft guns, 124 bombers and 145 fighters based at five fields. There were at least seven other major airfields on the island.

Even before the invasion of Bougainville, planes of the Fifth and Thirteenth Air Forces, together with Navy, Australian and New Zealand aircraft, conducted a devastating attack on New Britain and shattered Rabaul. Before the Marines completely conquered Bougainville, the Allied air forces had gained sufficient control of the air over New Britain to permit Army and Marine Corps troops to make landings at Cape Gloucester and Arawe, points near New Guinea.

The air assault on New Britain continued at a heavy pace through January and most of February of 1944, during which time the Allied air forces flew almost 6,000 sorties, leveling Rabaul and crushing Japanese resistance. Allied forces were able to make new landings on New Britain against only token opposition. As on Bougainville, segments of the Japanese defense were able to hold out for weeks, but by the end of February, most of New Britain was under Allied control. Rabaul, the long-feared Japanese strong point, was still in enemy hands, but no longer a strong point; air power alone had neutralized it.

*PHOTO RECONNAISSANCE OVER RABAUL, BY ROBERT LAESSIG.*

## FEAF Organized

On New Guinea, MacArthur's forces were still advancing to the northwest and there was a new air war in the offing. To support the ground movement, the Fifth Air Force had to gain air superiority over Hollandia in north central New Guinea, where there was a major concentration of Japanese strength.

Hollandia was several hundred miles from the Fifth's bases, but there was now available the long-range escort version of the P-38 and the fighters were able to provide cover all the way for the Fifth's B-24's, B-25's and A-20's. On March 30, and for the next three days, the Fifth conducted a series of heavy raids that almost completely wiped out Japanese air strength in the area. More than 300 planes were severely damaged on the ground and another 50 were destroyed in the air. It was in the Hollandia battle that the AAF produced its all-time ranking ace when Captain Richard Ira Bong topped Rickenbacker's World War I record by knocking down his 27th plane.

The ground forces quickly occupied Hollandia, then moved to the northwest to take the islands off the coast of New Guinea—Wakde, Biak and Noemfoor. Hollandia and the islands provided new bases for the continuing drive to the north.

In the Solomons, resistance had nearly ended and Allied aircraft were flying from bases in Bougainville. On New Guinea, there was still a large Japanese army, but it was cut off from supplies and reinforcements. There were still thousands of troops on New Britain and New Ireland, but they were similarly isolated. For all practical purposes, the whole South and Southwest Pacific was now Allied territory. It was time for the big step, the recapture of the Philippines.

For this campaign, the AAF units were reorganized, the Fifth and Thirteenth Air Forces combined into the Far East Air Forces under General Kenney. General Whitehead took over the Fifth, and the Thirteenth was now commanded by Major General St. Clair Streett. The Thirteenth moved from the Solomons to New Guinea and both air forces prepared for their assignments in the invasion of the Philippines.

*FIGHTER STRIP ON BOUGAINVILLE, BY ROBERT LAESSIG.*

*Leyte to Luzon*

Target for the initial invasion of the Philippines was Leyte, in the center of the Philippine chain. Once again the Far East Air Forces went through the now-familiar process of softening up the defenses by saturation raids, then supporting the assault.

On October 20, 1944, the American Sixth Army waded ashore into heavy opposition from some 20,000 Japanese defenders. There was equally stiff resistance in the air, and the FEAF planes were handicapped by the long distances from their southern bases to the battle area. But within a week the Army had taken sufficient ground for the engineers to crash-build a field at Tacloban. By the 28th, Fifth Air Force P-38's were operating from the strip and within the next two weeks there were several fields available to FEAF planes.

The complexion of the air battle changed swiftly. By the end of the year, the Fifth had shot down 314 enemy aircraft in the Leyte vicinity while losing only 16.

Planes of the FEAF pounded Japanese airfields throughout the islands incessantly. The enemy made a desperate effort to reinforce its air strength, sending planes to the Philippines by the hundreds, only to have them fall prey to the devastating Allied air attack. In all, some 1,500 Japanese planes were put out of action during the Philippine campaign.

MacArthur's troops invaded Mindoro, south of Manila, on December 15, then Lingayen on the main island of Luzon on January 9, 1945. By this time, Japanese air power was badly weakened; the enemy, forced to give up the air battle, evacuated most of its shattered Luzon air force.

*AIR SUPPLY IN THE PHILIPPINES, BY ROBERT LAESSIG.*

*Corregidor*

Aside from the *kamikazes*, which inflicted considerable damage on the invasion fleet, there was little air opposition as Allied ground forces swept through Luzon. The Fifth Air Force was able to concentrate on ground support operations, later described by the Joint Chiefs of Staff as ''strikingly effective.''

A key point in the Luzon campaign was the tiny island of Corregidor, a fortress guarding the approaches to Manila Bay. Before the war, American forces had built Corregidor into a major fortification, with underground battlements and tunnels. It was here that the Army had held off the Japanese attackers for six months in the black days of 1942. Now the Japanese were entrenched in the same position.

As preliminary to the capture of the island, planes of the Fifth, Seventh and Thirteenth Air Forces made a massive air assault, dropping on Corregidor more than 3,000 tons of bombs, the heaviest concentration ever delivered in the Southwest Pacific.

On February 16, the Fifth Air Force dropped the 503rd Parachute Regiment on the island, the drop heavily supported by air and naval firepower. As the paratroops secured a foothold, an amphibious landing was launched in another part of the island. The surface operations progressed smoothly, and by February 27, General MacArthur was able to halt air attacks against the island. On March 1, Manila Bay became an American anchorage and the issue of the Philippines was no longer in doubt.

In March and April, FEAF repaired and improved a number of airfields in Luzon, bringing into range of even the shorter-legged tactical aircraft Japan's major stronghold outside of the home islands—Formosa.

*BOMBING CORREGIDOR, BY ROBERT LAESSIG.*

*North to the Ryukyus*

In the recapture of the Philippines, Allied forces had by-passed strong enemy installations in the southern islands, in Borneo and in the Celebes. While United States forces were completing the conquest of Luzon, other Allied groups turned to the clean-up of the bypassed areas.

The Philippine island of Palawan was of particular importance in this campaign. It was invaded by an amphibious force on February 28, 1945 and within a month most of Palawan was under Allied control and its airfields were available for use. Palawan gave the AAF a valuable base for air attacks against Borneo and the Celebes, and, since it was the westernmost of the Philippines, it was strategically located for strikes against Japanese shipping in the South China Sea. From Palawan and other Philippine bases, the Fifth, Seventh and Thirteenth Air Forces waged an intensive air war against the enemy life-line, its shipping in the Sulu and South China Seas.

By spring, the tempo of the Pacific war had stepped up. From bases in Luzon, the FEAF conducted large-scale raids against Formosa, where the Japanese still had considerable air strength and from whence came a good portion of the *kamikaze* attacks on the American fleet. On April 1, 1945, an Army/Navy task force invaded Okinawa, foremost of the Ryukyu Islands. The resistance of the Japanese in this important battle was far greater than could have been expected of a rapidly crumpling power. Navy carrier aircraft provided the initial ground support until the availability of airstrips on the island permitted employment of a land-based tactical air force. This force was composed of AAF and Marine Corps squadrons, units of the Seventh Air Force under Brigadier General Thomas D. White making up the AAF complement.

On June 21, Okinawa fell and Allied engineers went to work to build a new airfield complex only 400 miles from Japan. The Fifth Air Force joined the Seventh in the Ryukyus and both initiated an all-out attack on Japanese shipping, on enemy installations in China and on the homeland itself: Kyushu, the most southern of the Japanese islands.

*AIR BASE AT PALAWAN IN THE PHILIPPINES, BY ROBERT LAESSIG.*

*China-Burma-India*

While Allied forces in the Pacific were leap-frogging from one island to another, the AAF was busily engaged on the Asian continent in the China-Burma-India theater of war. The combat elements of the AAF in CBI were the Tenth and Fourteenth Air Forces; in 1944, the Tenth was commanded by Brigadier General H. C. Davidson, the Fourteenth by Major General Claire L. Chennault, who had also headed the China Air Task Force from which the Fourteenth had been formed in 1943. Major General George E. Stratemeyer had overall command of all American air forces in the CBI.

A unique and amazing air operation in the CBI was the ''Hump'' operation of the AAF Air Transport Command. The Japanese conquest of Burma early in the war had severed the lifeline from India to China; hence, Allied forces in China had to be supplied by air. Flying over a poorly-mapped hump in the Himalayan chain, where peaks ran well over 16,000 feet, ATC crews battled terrain, cloud and frequent storms to keep the air lifeline open. Tonnages flown over the Hump were small to begin with, but the advent of the four-engine Douglas C-54 in substantial numbers sent delivery figures skyrocketing. From less than 3,000 tons a month in early 1943, ATC's effort climbed to 7,000 tons by October of that year and to 12,000 tons monthly during the first half of 1944. In mid-1945, ATC moved the incredible total of 71,000 tons over the Hump.

In 1944, the Tenth Air Force and the Royal Air Force wrested air superiority over Burma from the Japanese, then joined the British Fourteenth Army in a drive through Burma. The Tenth's B-24's hammered at Japanese supply depots and other behind-the-lines installations while its tactical units provided close support for the advancing British army. In May, 1945, the ground forces recaptured Rangoon and proceeded to eliminate Japanese forces from Burma.

A Japanese offensive in China in 1944 had resulted in the loss of most of the Fourteenth's forward bases, but in December of that year ATC and troop carrier units flew two complete divisions of Chinese troops from Burma to China. These fresh troops launched a counteroffensive in May, 1945, with the Fourteenth supplying close support. In short order the Allied ground forces recaptured the lost airfields, permitting Chennault's flyers to join the Fifth, Seventh and Thirteenth Air Forces in the mounting attack on the Japanese lifeline.

*SUPPLY LINE IN KUNMING, CHINA, BY LOREN FISHER.*

*The B-29 Bombardment of Japan*

The start of 1945 marked the beginning of an all-out strategic bombing attack on the home islands of Japan, using the new ''very heavy'' bomber, the Boeing B-29 Superfortress.

This giant of the air actually started operations months earlier from bases in China. The Twentieth Air Force—a unique organization in that it was personally headed by the commanding general of the AAF, General Arnold—had been created months earlier. Its major subdivisions were the XX and XXI Bomber Commands, and it was with the XX Bomber Command—initially under Brigadier General K. B. Wolfe and later Major General Curtis E. LeMay—that the B-29's first saw action. It was, however, limited action, designed less as an offensive threat than as a method of gaining experience with a brand new weapon system. From May, 1944, through March, 1945, XX Bomber Command averaged only two sorties per plane per month. The Command did drop some 800 tons of bombs on Japan proper, but most of its missions were against targets other than the homeland.

In June, 1944, a huge task force supported by heavy bombers of the Seventh and Thirteenth Air Forces invaded the Marianas—Saipan, Guam and Tinian—and in August the islands were secured. Immediately there started a massive program of airfield construction on these islands, some 1,500 miles from the main Japanese island of Honshu.

The first B-29's of Brigadier General Haywood S. Hansell Jr.'s XXI Bomber Command landed at Saipan on October 12 and, after a series of training missions against Pacific islands still occupied by the Japanese, the bombing of Japan from the Marianas got under way. On November 24, Brigadier General Emmett O'Donnell led his 73rd Wing in an attack on Tokyo, the first since the memorable Doolittle mission of 1942.

During the remainder of 1944 and the early days of 1945, Hansell's B-29's flew a number of raids against industrial targets in Japan with unexceptional results; there was a high ''abort'' rate, there were no bases from which escort fighters could operate, the weather was consistently bad and many B-29's, damaged over the targets, were forced to ditch in the ocean.

In January, 1945, General LeMay arrived in the Marianas to take over the XXI Bomber Command. In March, after four weeks of bloody fighting, the Marine Corps took the island of Iwo Jima and the engineers quickly constructed landing fields. Iwo Jima was of great importance to B-29 operations; roughly half-way between the Marianas and Japan, it served as an emergency landing area for the Superfortresses, some 2,400 of which touched down on the island during the remaining months of the war. Additionally, it provided a base from which fighters could escort the B-29's to Japan.

*B-24's OVER YAP, BY ROBERT LAESSIG.*

*V-J Day*

In March, 1945, LeMay's XXI Bomber Command initiated a strategy new to AAF bombardment operations: low level night attacks by incendiary laden B-29's. It was LeMay's decision to adopt the new technique and it was based on a number of factors—primary among them, intelligence reports that Japanese radar was not very effective, and that there were only two units of night-fighters in the home islands. Attack at low altitude would permit the B-29's to carry a heavier bomb load.

On March 9, 334 B-29's struck at Tokyo with incredible results; the raid destroyed about one of every four buildings in Tokyo and burned out almost 16 square miles. As anticipated, Japanese night defenses were inadequate and B-29 losses were low. In rapid succession, LeMay dispatched a repeat mission to Tokyo and strikes against Nagoya, Osaka and Kobe, the major industrial cities of Japan, with equally devastating results.

In July, General Spaatz arrived from Europe to take charge of all B-29 operations against Japan. By this time, the XX Bomber Command had moved to the Marianas and the Twentieth Air Force was further reinforced by B-29's from the United States. The Marianas force grew to almost 1,000 bombers and, to supplement it, the Eighth Air Force moved into the Ryukyus to conduct B-29 strikes from another direction.

Heavy bombers of General Kenney's Far East Air Forces, now based on Okinawa, joined the attack with strikes against ships, docks and warehouses, and the North American P-51 Mustangs slashed the Tokyo area with strafing attacks.

As Japan tottered under the massive air assault, MacArthur's troops moved into staging bases, preparing for a three-pronged invasion of the southernmost Japanese island, Kyushu. The invasion became unnecessary. On August 6, a B-29 of the Twentieth's 509th Composite Group took off from Tinian with the most destructive bomb load in history; six hours and 30 minutes later, the *Enola Gay*, piloted by Colonel Paul W. Tibbetts, Jr., dropped a nuclear bomb on the city of Hiroshima, killing more than 35,000 persons. On August 9, the B-29 *Bock's Car* commanded by Major Charles W. Sweeney, dropped a second A-bomb on Nagasaki.

On August 14, the Twentieth Air Force staged the heaviest one-day air assault of the Pacific war, when 828 bombers escorted by 186 fighters, rained 6,000 tons of incendiary and demolition bombs on what remained of Japan's industrial capacity.

President Truman announced the unconditional surrender of the Japanese government before the last B-29 had returned.

*B-24's RETURNING FROM A MISSION, BY ROBERT LAESSIG.*

*A Chapter Closed*

The end of World War II marked another great chapter in the history of America's air arm, one of glory and unqualified success. The air victory had cost dearly; some 40,000 airmen of the AAF lost their lives. The AAF, however, had demonstrated conclusively that military aviation was no longer an experiment, but, rather, a new dimension in warfare.

During the war against Japan, planes of the AAF flew slightly more than 669,000 sorties, the Twentieth Air Force contributing about 40,000 of them. Of more than 650,000 tons of bombs dropped by all Allied air forces, the AAF delivered about half a million tons.

There were many differences between the types of air operations flown in the Pacific and those conducted in Europe, but the differences served to point up the great versatility of the AAF.

History had been made, but even more important, the pressure of combat had accelerated the growth of both concepts and tactic, idea and execution. The Army Air Forces had responded to the call, measured up to the challenge, and emerged with a clear goal for the future.

GENERAL H. H. ARNOLD, BY GERALD BROCKHURST.

CHAPTER V

# The Post-War Years

*The Independent Air Arm*

With the end of the war, there came a sharp decline in the strength of the AAF. During the 21 months after V-J Day, the AAF melted away. The personnel force dropped from more than 2,250,000 officers and enlisted men to slightly more than 300,000. The unit strength fell off from 218 groups to 52— but of these, 50 could hardly be termed "combat ready." They were undermanned, poorly equipped, inadequately supplied and woefully lacking in maintenance capability.

The downward trend was halted in March, 1947, with the issuance of the Truman Doctrine. It had become evident that there existed a so-called "cold war" with the forces of Communism, and the Truman Doctrine was affirmation of a national policy to provide aid to peoples of the world threatened by Communist aggression. The key to such a policy was the ability of the United States to deliver the atomic bomb should it again become necessary. This resulted in a limited build-up of AAF strength, striving toward a goal of 70 combat-effective groups.

The growth of a force-in-being was slow, but there was considerable activity on the development front. In 1947, the AAF was experimenting with primitive missiles and high-altitude rockets and preparing for an attack on the sound barrier with a special research airplane, the Bell XS-1. Most notable was the advent of the jet airplane, a wartime research project. The Lockheed P-80 and the Republic P-84 jet fighters went into operational service and the North American P-86 was being readied for its first flight late in 1947. Other fighters were in development, and jet propulsion was being extended to bombardment aircraft like the North American B-45, Consolidated Vultee XB-46, Boeing XB-47, Martin XB-48 and Northrop XB-49 Flying Wing. In an early stage of development was the superjet, the Boeing XB-52, and for the interim the AAF was operating a propeller-driven bomber capable of flying 5,000 miles non-stop, the Consolidated Vultee B-36.

On September 18, the air arm realized a dream that had started with Foulois and Mitchell and been carried forward by other leaders from Patrick to Arnold and Spaatz—the independent air force. The Congress created a separate Department of the Air Force and an operating entity, the United States Air Force. W. Stuart Symington was named Secretary of the Air Force and General Carl A. Spaatz, who had succeeded General Arnold as commanding general of the AAF, became the first Chief of Staff of the USAF.

*GENERAL CARL A. SPAATZ, BY THOMAS E. STEPHENS. Wartime leader Spaatz became the first Chief of Staff of the Air Force on September 18, 1947.*

*New Plans and a New Chief*

In the months following the Congressional grant of autonomy to the Air Force, the research and development projects initiated during and immediately after the war began to bear fruit. A most notable achievement was the first flight at a speed faster than sound, made on October 14, 1947, by USAF Captain Charles E. Yeager in the Bell XS-1. November and December saw the initial test flights of two airplanes which were to play important roles in Air Force history, the Boeing B-47 and North American P-86 (it was still ''P-86'' at the time of its first flight, but within a few months it was to become ''F-86'' as the USAF abandoned the old ''pursuit'' designation in favor of ''fighter''). The Air Force also started tests of what was then a mammoth airplane, the Consolidated Vultee XC-99, a transport version of the B-36.

The USAF command structure was similar to that of the AAF, with three basic functional commands—Strategic Air Command, Tactical Air Command and Air Defense Command—backed by five support commands and five overseas commands. To these were later added the Air Research and Development Command and Continental Air Command. In February, 1948, the USAF's Air Transport Command was merged with the Naval Air Transport Service to form Military Air Transport Service under USAF Major General Laurence S. Kuter.

In April, General Hoyt S. Vandenberg succeeded General Spaatz as Chief of Staff. Then, in June, came an international impasse which was to involve the Air Force in one of its most memorable peacetime operations. The partition of Germany at the end of the war had made the city of Berlin an island in the midst of the Soviet Zone of occupation. On June 22, 1948, the Soviets cut off all rail, barge and highway traffic into Berlin, isolating the city and its American, British and French zones. Faced with the prospect of abandoning the city to the Soviets, the western nations chose a dramatic alternative: complete supply of a city of 2,000,000 people by air. The historic air supply mission became variously known as the Berlin Air Lift, Operation Plainfare and Operation Vittles.

GENERAL HOYT S. VANDENBERG,
BY FRANCIS BEAUGUREAU.

*The Berlin Air Lift*

The Air Lift got under way four days after the start of the surface blockade. Douglas C-47's of General LeMay's United States Air Forces in Europe flew 80 tons of food and medicine from Wiesbaden to Berlin's Tempelhof Airdrome. It was a good effort, but a far cry from the amount needed to supply the city—4,500 tons a day.

Additional planes and crews were flown into Germany and the availability of the bigger Douglas C-54 boosted the lift capability. By the end of July, the USAF was freighting more than 2,000 tons a day to Berlin and the British were providing an additional several hundred tons. At that time the Air Force set up the 1st Airlift Task Force, headed by a veteran of the wartime Hump lift, Major General William H. Tunner, (this later became the Combined Airlift Task Force, embracing the effort of the British as well as the USAF).

Eventually there were more than 300 C-54's in the airlift fleet, together with the British aircraft and lesser numbers of special purpose planes like the Douglas C-74 and the Fairchild C-82. The number of fields was also expanded, until there were four at the loading end of the run and three—Gatow and Tegel as well as Tempelhof—in Berlin. Tonnage flown mounted steadily until, at the start of 1949, it was running about 10,000 tons a day and it became possible to increase the food ration of the people of West Berlin. About two-thirds of all the tonnage was coal, and in addition to food, the airlift delivered commercial and industrial items, liquid fuel, medical supplies and even newsprint.

The deliveries were not easy, however. The planes had to fly into Berlin in three narrow corridors, a factor which created an air traffic control problem. Continual utilization of the planes made maintenance very difficult. Bad weather frequently made trouble for, the lift, but never stalled it completely. In the "Easter Parade" lift of April, there were almost 1,400 landings in Berlin in a single day and tonnage reached a record 12,940. A month later the Soviets lifted the blockade, but the task force continued to operate until September 30, 1949, to build up reserve stores in Berlin. In the 15 months of the lift, planes of the Vittles task force delivered 2,325,000 tons of supplies to Berlin. Air power had scored an impressive victory in the cold war.

112

*RETURN FOR A RELOAD, BY HERB MOTT. A MATS transport makes a night landing at Rhein Main airport, where it is quickly reloaded and dispatched again to Berlin in the 'round-the-clock operation known as the Berlin Air Lift.*

*War in Korea*

In January, 1950, the Atomic Energy Commission, by Presidential directive, intensified its research on thermonuclear weapons. In a coordinated effort, the USAF started to prepare for delivery of such weapons, not only by bomber but by unmanned systems. The Air Force was studying long-range ballistic missiles preparatory to awarding a contract for development of an intercontinental missile.

In April, New York attorney Thomas K. Finletter succeeded W. Stuart Symington as Secretary of the Air Force; General Vandenberg continued as Chief of Staff. Two months later the Air Force found itself in another war, this time in a country which few Americans could accurately locate— Korea. After the Japanese surrender in 1945, Korea had been partitioned at the 38th parallel of latitude, with Soviet forces occupying the northern section of the country and American troops the southern part. South Korea became the Republic of Korea in 1948 and the United States withdrew its occupation force, with the exception of a military advisory group, in 1949. In the north, the Soviets and Communist China had created the People's Democratic Republic of Korea, and there was continuing friction between the two Korean groups. This friction erupted into war in June 25, 1950, when the North Koreans, supplied by the Soviets and aided by complete Chinese military units, invaded South Korea. The Security Council of the United Nations passed a resolution calling for provision of assistance to the Republic of Korea. The UN set up a United Nations Command, headed by General MacArthur and composed of United States, British, Australian, Turkish and other forces. Conduct of the air war fell to the USAF's Far East Air Forces under Lieutenant General George E. Stratemeyer; air units of the other UN countries were absorbed by FEAF.

At the outset, FEAF was not a strong air force. It had a few squadrons of F-80 jet fighters, but the bulk of its strength was in propeller-driven aircraft: Boeing B-29's and Douglas B-26's, and North American F-51 and F-82 fighters. FEAF's primary assignment in the early days of the war was close battlefield support as United States and ROK forces attempted to stop the drive of the North Korean troops toward the south.

*ARMAMENT CREWS LOADING F-15's IN KOREA, BY FRANCIS BEAUGUREAU. At the outset of the Korean war the bulk of FEAF's strength was in propeller-driven aircraft.*

*The Pusan Perimeter*

The prime USAF organizations in the early days of the war were Major General Emmett O'Donnell, Jr.'s FEAF Bomber Command and Major General Earle E. Partridge's Fifth Air Force, flying from bases in Japan. The B-29's were used primarily for ground support work and in the first month of the action well over 60 percent of FEAF's total sorties were flown in battlefield support.

Badly outnumbered, United States and ROK forces were driven deep into South Korea in the first weeks of the war, but even in the ground retreat FEAF performed effectively. Said Major General William F. Dean, commanding the 24th Infantry Division: ''Without question, the Air Force definitely blunted the initial North Korean thrust to the southward. Without this continuing air effort, it is doubtful if the courageous combat soldiers, spread thinly along the line, could have withstood the vastly numerically superior enemy.''

The American Eighth Army dug into positions forming a perimeter around the South Korean port of Pusan and fought off repeated enemy attacks, aided by intensive close support operations flown by FEAF and Navy carrier-based aircraft.

Strengthened by reinforcements from the United States, FEAF waged a furious air war in an effort to gain air supremacy over South Korea. They achieved it in short order, because the Communists had counted on massive troop superiority and they had little in the way of an air force. By August 10, pilots of the UN Command had destroyed 110 enemy aircraft, leaving the North Koreans with perhaps a score of flyable planes.

Now FEAF went to work in a large-scale interdiction campaign, smashing supply lines and depots far to the north of the battle line, striking troop columns attempting to reinforce the drive toward Pusan. By the end of August, this campaign had all but stopped the flow of supplies and reinforcements to the perimeter area. The North Koreans made one last-ditch attempt to break through to Pusan, but again they were repulsed. Close support missions flown by the Fifth Air Force, the B-29's and the Navy figured importantly in this action.

*F-80's OVER A TARGET IN KOREA, BY FRANCIS BEAUGUREAU.*
*The F-80 was the first USAF jet to be employed in combat.*

*Strategic Bombing in Korea*

In August, Strategic Air Command sent two additional groups of B-29's to beef up FEAF Bomber Command, and FEAF initiated a heavy strategic bombardment attack against North Korea. The North Korean army was getting most of its war supplies from the Soviet Union and China, and the supply sources were located north of the Yalu River in Manchuria. FEAF, however, was prevented by Presidential order from sending attacks beyond the Yalu.

There were, nonetheless, some industrial areas in North Korea—notably Pyongyang, Chongjin, Wonsan and Hungnam—which were providing war materiel, and FEAF directed its attention to these targets. Initially, FEAF considered the use of incendiary bombs, so effective against Japan in World War II, against these cities. But U.S./UN concern for the civilian population resulted in employment of standard high explosive stores instead of the fire-bombs.

Throughout the month, O'Donnell's B-29's ranged over the industrial targets in a series of massive area bombardment raids, flying ''maximum effort'' missions and delivering astonishingly large tonnages of destruction; in fact, FEAF topped World War II records for sorties per plane and tons delivered per plane, although the numbers of planes over target were small by comparison with World War II standards.

In less than two months, North Korea's industry was reduced to a mass of rubble. On September 15, General Stratemeyer reported that ''practically all of the major military industrial targets strategically important to the enemy forces and to their war potential have now been neutralized.'' On September 26, the Joint Chiefs of Staff ordered a suspension of the strategic bombing offensive.

*RUBBLE IN KOREA, BY DAVID HALL.*

*The 38th Parallel*

General MacArthur's forces made an amphibious landing on September 15 at Inchon on the west coast of Korea, well to the north of the Pusan perimeter. The following day, the United States Eighth Army, supported by the Fifth Air Force, broke out of the perimeter and started a drive to the north. Cargo re-supply for both the break-out and the amphibious landing was provided by the newly-created FEAF Combat Cargo Command, headed by General Tunner of Berlin Air Lift fame.

North Korean opposition crumpled and Allied forces moved swiftly through South Korea, aided by air support from FEAF, the 1st Marine Air Wing and Navy carrier-based aircraft. It took only 11 days for the Eighth Army to link up with the amphibious force, and, at the same time, ROK units on the east coast were driving toward the 38th parallel. On September 29 the ROK government returned to its capital city of Seoul.

Now MacArthur launched an offensive against North Korea, the Fifth Air Force moving into bases in Korea to support the drive from airfields closer to the front lines. On October 19, the Eighth Army and the ROK, covered by fighters of the Fifth, took Pyongyang, the North Korean capital. On the following day, Combat Cargo Command dropped almost 3,000 paratroops and more than 300 tons of equipment at Sukchon and Sunchon, north of Pyongyang. Aided by a ''softening up'' attack of 140 FEAF planes, the drop was completely successful and the paratroops cut off a main artery to the north.

The land forces moved farther into North Korea and were advancing toward the Manchurian border when the Chinese intervened on November 26. The Chinese threw tremendous ground forces into the battle, and, once again badly outnumbered, the UN troops were forced to retreat into South Korea. In the spring of 1951, the Chinese started two major drives designed to eliminate UN forces from all of Korea, but both were stalled. FEAF bombing attacks and close support contributed in great measure to halting these drives. In May and June, the UN forces counterattacked and moved northward to a line close to the 38th parallel. On June 23 the Soviets proposed negotiations toward a truce and the UN accepted.

*BOMB DUMP IN KOREA, BY DAVID HALL.*

*MiG Alley*

The truce talks, which started on July 10, 1951, did not result in an immediate cease-fire; they were to continue for two years. Ground fighting continued, but it was mostly on a unit action basis rather than engagements of major forces. The Korean war became primarily an air war.

In the meantime, there had been some top level personnel changes. General Matthew B. Ridgway took over the UN Command; Lieutenant General O. P. Weyland became commander of the Far East Air Forces; Lieutenant General Frank F. Everest was named Fifth Air Force Commander.

On September 1, 1951, the Communists initiated an all-out campaign designed to gain air superiority over Korea. At that time, intelligence estimates credited the Communist forces with about 1,250 aircraft, including well over 500 of the highly-maneuverable, Soviet-built MiG-15's, planes which were far superior to all USAF aircraft in the theater except the North American F-86 Sabre, of which the FEAF had only 105.

FEAF forces were engaged in a large-scale interdiction program, the B-29's, medium bombers and fighter-bombers concentrating on the North Korean railway transportation system, the F-86's screening the attacks. But, starting in September, the Communists sent such great numbers of MiG's into battle that the outnumbered F-86's could not contain them. They evaded or broke through the screens and were able to destroy many of the interdicting bombers.

FEAF was now able to equip a second wing of F-86's, but the odds did not change as the Communists added more MiG's. A furious air battle raged over North Korea, a lot of the action taking place in the area between the Yalu and Chongchon Rivers, a sector which became known as "MiG Alley."

Since the MiG's were day fighters, the B-29's started night operations, using Shoran bombing, and in November they conducted a number of strikes against enemy airfields without loss. The railway interdiction campaign became a 'round-the-clock operation, the fighter-bombers attacking during the day, the B-29's ranging over the same targets at night, as the 500,000-man Communist labor force desperately tried to repair the damage.

FEAF continued the war of interdiction until May, 1952. It was highly effective but it could not be termed completely successful. The Communists had emplaced such heavy anti-aircraft defenses in key areas that losses were heavy; weather also hampered the effort and FEAF furthered suffered from lack of a strike force sufficiently large for the task. Nonetheless, a major objective had been attained; the battering delivered to the railway system made it unable to support a major new ground offensive.

And FEAF had also thwarted the efforts of the Communists to gain air superiority. The F-86 pilots, substituting skill and training for force in numbers, had negated the MiG threat and by mid-1952 the Chinese MiG pilots had lost their enthusiasm for engaging the Sabres.

*RADAR-DIRECTED
SABREJETS,
BY WARREN KING.*

## The Air Pressure Campaign and Armistice

In July, 1952, FEAF started a new ''air pressure campaign,'' the aim of which was to make the war as costly as possible to the Communists through continuous destruction of troops, facilities, equipment and supplies. The major goal was air superiority over all of Korea and destruction of the Red Air Force; secondly, FEAF was to inflict maximum damage on a wide selection of ground targets.

The Fifth Air Force, now under Lieutenant General Glenn O. Barcus, was strengthened by the arrival of the new F-86F, an improved version of the earlier Sabre. As the air pressure program got under way and FEAF began smashing targets near the Yalu, the Communist air force made a furious effort to counter the attack. MiG Alley, quiet for months, became the scene of a tremendous new air battle. Once again pilots of the Fifth prevailed; in September the F-86's destroyed 63 MiG's while suffering only six losses.

The autumn battle dulled the Chinese desire for combat. Throughout the winter months they elected not to fight the Sabre pilots and raced for the safety of Manchuria when taken by surprise. They suddenly became aggressive again in May, 1953, and launched new attacks against FEAF's ''air pressuring'' bombers. But by this time the Fifth Air Force's Sabre pilots completely dominated the air. In May the Fifth wiped out 56 MiG's, in June, 75 and in July, another 32. Throughout this period, only one F-86 was lost— and its pilot was rescued.

By June it appeared that the lengthy truce talks were on the verge of success, but as they neared an end the Communists launched one last ground attack against the Eighth Army near Kumhwa, in central Korea. Lieutenant General Samuel E. Anderson, now heading the Fifth, ordered an all-out effort against the Communist army. The Fifth, together with the Navy, provided a tremendous concentration of air support that helped the Eighth Army stall the final attack.

In the last week of the war, practically all of FEAF's units were engaged in attacks on the enemy airfields in North Korea. In one raid, B-29's wiped out 36 MiG's on the ground; there were few MiG sightings in the air. Captain Ralph Parr, a double ace, shot down a Red transport on July 27 for the last ''kill'' of the war. A reconnaissance mission on that day showed that there was not one serviceable airfield left in Korea. The armistice was signed on July 27 and the cease-fire went into effect that evening.

*COLONEL DEAN HESS AND KOREAN WAR ORPHANS, BY REYNOLD BROWN. Dean Hess is a symbol of the humanitarian aspect of the USAF and its people. Hess, who studied for the ministry before entering the Air Force and becoming an ace in Korea, set up an orphanage for homeless Korean children.*

*Mission Accomplished*

In the course of slightly more than three years of action in Korea, Far East Air Forces flew 721,000 sorties and delivered 476,000 tons of explosives against the Communists. This was a tremendous record, in view of the relatively small size of the force available to air commanders. Average strength of FEAF throughout the war was 19 groups and 62 squadrons totaling about 1,250 aircraft. Peak strength, reached in the summer of 1952, was 20 groups and 70 squadrons with 1,441 planes.

Although it had not won a clear-cut victory in Korea, the United States had resisted aggression. Its Air Force, however, could certainly lay claim to victory in the skies. FEAF had seized and maintained air superiority against heavy odds; the Sabre pilots had outfought the enemy MiG's and rolled up a kill ratio of better than ten to one. The Bomber Command, despite target restrictions, had proved an extremely effective force, particularly in the air pressure campaign of the last year of the war. The fighter-bombers and other close support units of FEAF had figured prominently in the successes of the UN ground forces.

In its first jet war, the Air Force had demonstrated a great degree of versatility in a peculiar type of war and had once again shown the importance of air superiority in any kind of conflict. General Weyland wrote: "There is little doubt in my mind that the outcome of the conflict would have been vastly different had enemy domination of the air reversed the military positions of the Communists and the United Nations Command."

While the war was still in progress, there were developments on the home front. Harold E. Talbott had succeeded Thomas K. Finletter as Secretary of the Air Force on February 4, 1953 and General Nathan F. Twining took over from General Vandenberg as Chief of Staff. The USAF was moving toward an all-jet combat force. In production were three new high-performance fighters: the North American F-100, successor to the Sabre; the McDonnell F-101; and the Convair F-102. In March, 1953, the Air Force took delivery of its last propeller-driven bomber, a Boeing TB-50H advanced Superfortress. Mainstay of the long-range bombardment force was the Convair B-36, but the eight-jet B-52 was in development. Already in operational service and in large-scale production was the Boeing B-47, the standard medium bomber.

GLOBAL POWER, BY DEAN FAUSETT.

*Post-Korea Gains*

From a low point of 48 combat and troop carrier wings at the outbreak of war in Korea, the strength of the USAF had climbed steadily until, at the time General Twining became Chief of Staff, it reached 106 wings. The build-up had been due, however, to the demands of war and the possibility of its escalation.

In mid-1953, the Joint Chiefs of Staff were taking a long look at the existing and planned strength levels of all the services. General Twining played an important part in gaining Department of Defense approval for a new Air Force program, adopted in the fall of 1953, which called for further expansion to a goal of 137 wings.

Although he was a firm believer in a continuing high level of research and development, General Twining was particularly aware of the human factor in air operations, and he sought better methods of training for the high skill levels the modern USAF needed. ''We speak continually of the importance of scientific and technological breakthroughs,'' he said. ''I know of no single breakthrough that I would trade for the assurance that the USAF would get—and be able to keep—the skilled men it needs in the years ahead.''

There was considerable activity in the research and development area during the latter months of 1953. On September 1, the Air Force advanced another step in the technique of aerial refueling, pioneered in the twenties, when a B-47 was refueled by a KB-47 tanker in the first jet-to-jet fuel transfer. On October 10, the X-10 ramjet-powered test vehicle, prototype of a planned long-range missile named Navaho, made its initial flight. Later the same month, the F-102 supersonic fighter flew for the first time. On December 12, Major Charles E. Yeager, the first faster-than-sound pilot, flew the Bell X-1A research plane to a speed of 1,612 miles per hour, another research step toward the double-sonic aircraft that were to join the operational USAF within a few years.

GENERAL NATHAN F. TWINING, BY SANDOR KLEIN.

*Start of the Missile Era*

On February 10, 1954, the Air Force Strategic Missiles Evaluation Committee under Dr. John von Neumann reported the possibility of a major technological breakthrough which would permit develop-ment of thermonuclear warheads small enough to be missile-delivered over long distances. The com-mittee also reported that other technical problems connected with development of an intercontinental ballistic missile could be resolved within a few years, and it recommended that the Air Force organize a special development/management group to accelerate Project Atlas, the USAF's long-range ballistic missile program. Accordingly, the Air Force created a USAF Western Development Division (later the Ballistic Missile Division), headed by Brigadier General Bernard A. Schriever.

In addition to the ICBM, the USAF was working on development of missiles of several types. Besides the ballistic type of missile, there was the pilotless bomber variety, a winged, air-breathing vehicle powered by jet propulsion. The first such weapons were already in being; the Martin TM-61 Matador, which had been in test status since 1949, was deployed to Germany with the 1st Tactical Missile Squadron in March, 1954. In development were long-range strategic versions of the pilotless bomber, the Northrop SM-62 Snark and the North American SM-64 Navaho. The USAF was also developing a pilotless fighter for interception missions, an air-to-surface missile for extension of the capabilities of the manned bomber fleet, and air-to-air missiles for use by manned interceptors.

Another new USAF airplane made its debut. On February 9, 1954, the Lockheed XF-104 air superiority fighter, capable of speeds more than twice that of sound, took to the air on its initial flight. The Air Force placed production orders for this fourth member of the ''Century Series'' of fighters.

*Overseas Bases*

During the early fifties, the Air Force further expanded its overseas operations. From the end of World War II the Air Force had maintained bases in Europe and the Pacific, operated by USAFE and FEAF respectively. There had, of course, been considerable base expansion in the Far East during the Korean war and many of the new fields were kept active after cessation of hostilities.

Strategic Air Command had a particular need for overseas sites. The command's intercontinental B-36's were based in the United States, but the B-36's were relatively few in number; the real mainstay of the SAC strike force was the fleet of shorter-ranging B-47's, which, even with in-flight refueling, required bases abroad to meet the nation's defense commitments in the cold war. In 1948, the United States had made an agreement with the United Kingdom which allowed basing of SAC bombers in England. Two years later, the government concluded additional agreements which permitted construction of SAC bases in Thule, Greenland, in Spain and North Africa; and in 1954, SAC strengthened its capability in the Far East when it assigned the 3rd Air Division to Guam. At this time SAC was also operating the 7th Air Division in England and the 5th Air Division in Morocco. In addition to these permanently-emplaced forces, SAC ran rotational missions on a regular basis to Europe, the Far East, North Africa, Alaska and Greenland.

Tactical Air Command also started rotational flights in 1964, sending its fighter-bomber and troop carrier wings to Europe for six-month periods of duty with USAFE.

The Military Air Transport Service was operating all over the world. From its terminal at McGuire AFB, New Jersey, MATS flew to Europe, North Africa and the Middle East; Travis AFB, California, served as the gateway to the East. Global operations required a huge network of bases, some of which were directly controlled by MATS, others by joint U.S./foreign authority and still others under the direction of private contractors.

NOUASSEUR AIR BASE IN NORTH AFRICA, BY BOB McCALL.

*Debut of the B-52*

The USAF reached a milestone in weapon system progress in August, 1954, when Boeing began delivering production models of the B-52, which had been flying in experimental status since 1952. The mighty, eight-jet bomber, which could fly intercontinental distances without in-flight refueling, as well as reach any point on the globe with the aid of aerial tankers, was an important addition to SAC's deterrent force. And, even as the first Stratofortresses were rolling off the production line, designers were working on more advanced versions of the plane that would go faster and farther.

Looking to the future, the USAF continued the rocketplane research program that had started with the X-1. There was now available a test vehicle with performance capabilities far beyond those of the X-1: the Bell X-2, designed for altitudes of more than 100,000 feet and speeds of more than 2,000 miles per hour. On August 5, Lieutenant Colonel Frank K. Everest, Jr. piloted the X-2 on its first glide flight.

But even the fantastic speed and altitude capabilities of the X-2 represented only moderate performance in the view of USAF planners, who could see a ''someday'' requirement for a hypersonic aircraft, one which could fly at a speed five times that of sound. On December 23, 1954, the partners in the X-1 and X-2 programs—the USAF, the Navy and the National Advisory Committee for Aeronautics—signed a ''memorandum of understanding'' on a ''Joint Project for a New High Speed Research Airplane,'' a vehicle which was to carry the designation X-15. In the last week of the year, the Air Force opened a design competition for the new research craft, for which the USAF had the responsibility of supervising design and construction.

PORTRAIT OF A B-52, BY KEITH FERRIS.

*The Air Force Academy*

The year 1955 was an extremely active one on the research and development front.

In January, the Department of Defense officially announced the existence of the ICBM program and confirmed that the Atlas missile was already being built by the Convair Division of General Dynamics Corporation. In April, the USAF approved proposals by its Western Development Division for the start of a second ICBM program, the weapon to be known as the Titan (Martin Company later received the prime contract for Titan development). In December, the USAF awarded a contract to Douglas Aircraft Company for its first intermediate-range ballistic missile, Thor.

There was also progress on another type of missile, the air-to-air rocket with an atomic warhead. The Douglas Genie, launched from a B-36 on April 6, was exploded six miles in the air over Yucca Flats, Nevada.

Among the USAF's early space experiments were a series of flights designed to probe the effects of weightlessness on humans; this project got under way July 1 at the School of Aviation Medicine.

In September, the USAF awarded the development contract for the X-15 to North American Aviation. Then, on October 22, the YF-104A, with Russell M. Roth at the controls, exceeded Mach 1. On November 18, Colonel Everest took the X-2 aloft on its first powered flight, and four days later, the Republic XF-105 flew faster than sound on its first flight.

The year was also notable for the achievement of a long-time dream of Air Force leaders: the Air Force Academy. For more than a decade, the USAF had sought such an establishment, but it was not until March, 1954, that the legislation was passed. In June, 1954, a commission selected a site near Colorado Springs, Colorado, as the academy's permanent home, but until the facilities could be built, a temporary location was provided at Lowry AFB, Colorado. Lieutenant General Hubert R. Harmon was named first superintendent of the academy, which admitted its first class of 300 cadets in July, 1955. On July 11, Secretary Talbott formally dedicated the Air Force Academy. It was one of his last public acts; he resigned on August 1, 1955 and was succeeded by his Assistant Secretary for Research and Development, Donald A. Quarles.

DEDICATION OF THE AIR FORCE ACADEMY CHAPEL, BY MARIO COOPER.

*Progress in Air Defense*

At the start of the decade of the fifties, an era of rapidly advancing technology, the Air Force still had one major defect in its air defense system: radar coverage over the North American continent was spotty, and over the seaward flanks and the polar regions it was non-existent.

As an early remedial step, the United States had concluded an agreement with the government of Canada in 1951 providing for construction of a chain of jointly-operated radar stations across southern Canada. The Pinetree Line, consisting of 30 stations, was completed late in 1955.

Long before its completion, however, USAF leaders recognized that it was only a partial solution. There was still a need for a system which could pick up invading aircraft far to the north and provide an earlier warning than Pinetree could give.

Another joint agreement, signed in 1954, called for two additional radar lines. The Canadian government agreed to build a mid-Canada line; the United States would set up a chain of radars above the Arctic Circle to be known as the Distant Early Warning (DEW) Line.

Construction began early in 1955 on a chain of radar stations located along a 3,000-mile arc running from Alaska through northern Canada and Greenland. By August 1, 1957, the DEW Line was operational.

To provide warning of attack over the seas, the USAF teamed with the Navy in a three-way approach to the problem. The Navy would operate a number of radar-equipped picket ships off each coast. The ships would be supplemented by squadrons of long-ranging airborne early warning and control aircraft; (the USAF organized several AEWGC squadrons on each coast and equipped them with Lockheed RC-121 Super Constellations). A third warning device was the man-made radar island, or ''Texas Tower,'' as it came to be known. The first of three USAF Texas Towers became operational in December, 1955.

To tie together the data from all the stations, process it quickly and disseminate the information to air defense units, the Air Force developed an electronic system named SAGE, for Semi-Automatic Ground Environment. SAGE's computers could receive, store and display information on all air traffic over North America, and, in the event the ''traffic'' was hostile, provide an electronic means of controlling defending aircraft.

NORTHERN LIGHTS FROM FROBISHER BAY, BAFFIN ISLAND, BY CARL BROEMEL. At this eastern anchorage of the DEW Line, says artist Broemel, the primitive minds of the Eskimos are awed by nature's great display of heavenly lights, but they have little interest in the man-made wonders—airplane and radar station— which have become familiar sights in the far northland.

*Advances in Research*

Although the long-range, air-breathing pilotless bomber type of missile was later to be outmoded by the ballistic missile, it was still an important alternate avenue of approach in 1956, when the Atlas was in an early development stage. Hence, there was great jubilation at the Air Force Missile Test Center, Florida, on January 13, 1956, when the Northrop Snark successfully completed a 2,000 mile flight down-range. But Snark was destined to have only a brief Air Force career in later years, and its companion, Navaho, was to be canceled altogether. Snark and Navaho were victims of rapidly expanding military science and technology, which was accelerating at an amazing pace in 1956.

The Air Force played the leading role in the joint military/ Atomic Energy Commission nuclear tests of 1956. On May 21, a B-52 dropped the first airborne H-bomb, which exploded in the air over Bikini Atoll in the Pacific.

In the X-2 program, performance records were being shattered on almost every flight. On July 23, Colonel Everest flew the rocket-powered plane to a new top speed of slightly more than 1,900 miles per hour. Everest's back-up pilot, Captain Iven C. Kincheloe, set a new altitude record on September 7 when he took the X-2 to a height of 126,000 feet.

But, only three weeks later, the X-2 project came to a sudden and tragic end on the 13th flight of the research craft. Captain Milburn G. Apt piloted the plane to another new record speed, 2,094 miles per hour. But, at the peak of its trajectory, the X-2 became violently uncontrollable. Apt ejected the escape capsule but was killed as it struck the desert floor. Since an earlier crash had destroyed the only other model of the X-2, the project was terminated.

Late in the year, the Air Force reached a new plateau in the development of bombardment aircraft. On November 11, the Convair B-58, the first supersonic bomber, successfully completed its first test flight.

*B-58 AT EDWARDS AIR FORCE BASE, BY WALTER RICHARDS.*

*New Leadership*

The range capability of the Boeing B-52 was dramatically pointed up early in 1957 when the USAF conducted the first nonstop jet flight around the world. During January 16–18, three B-52's made the global circuit in 45 hours and 20 minutes. And, in the same month, SAC was further strengthened by the entry into operational service of the first Boeing KC-135 jet Stratotankers.

Air Defense Command received a similar boost. The Boeing IM-99 Bomarc, a pilotless interceptor of double-sonic speed, was ordered into production for use in long-range area defense.

There were two notable balloon flights in June. On the first, Captain Joseph W. Kittinger, Jr. made the first solo balloon flight into the stratosphere, reaching an altitude of 96,000 feet in Man High I, a plastic balloon. Kittinger was aloft for more than six and a half hours, and he spent two hours above 92,000 feet.

Later in the month, the USAF launched a space research program, Project Farside. The world's largest balloon carried more than a ton of instruments to an altitude of 104,000 feet.

There were failures mixed with the successes. Two attempts to fire the Thor IRBM were unsuccessful and on June 11, when the USAF tried to test the first model of the Atlas ICBM, it became necessary to destroy the missile at an altitude of 5,000 feet.

The first half of 1957 saw a double change in the Air Force's leadership. On May 1, Donald A. Quarles became Deputy Secretary of Defense; he was succeeded as Secretary of the Air Force by James H. Douglas, Jr., who had served for four years as Under Secretary. And on July 1, General Thomas D. White took over the USAF command as Chief of Staff. General Twining was appointed by President Eisenhower as Chairman of the Joint Chiefs of Staff.

*The ICBM Arrives*

''There is a far better way to protect our homes and our people than to fight and win a great war,'' said Chief of Staff General Thomas D. White. ''The better way is to be so obviously superior in our ability to carry the war to an enemy that he will not take the risk of starting one.''

When General White assumed leadership of the Air Force, the United States enjoyed a measure of superiority in the air over the major potential aggressor, the Soviet Union. The USSR could not match the striking power of the USAF's Strategic Air Command, and SAC's deterrent power was backed by a modern fleet of air defense, tactical and support aircraft.

But technology had introduced a new element to air warfare. On August 26, 1957, the Soviet news agency *Tass* proudly announced that the USSR had successfully launched a ''super long distance intercontinental multistage ballistic rocket.'' A few days later the Department of Defense confirmed that the Soviets had tested not one, but four to six ICBM's earlier that year.

The initial failures of the USAF's ballistic missiles now loomed doubly important. Continuation of the strategic deterrence policy demanded that these weapons be brought to early operational status.

The Air Force and its contractors rebounded from the failures. On September 20, the Thor IRBM achieved its first test success and by year-end it had made four flawless flights. The weapon was ordered into production late in November, along with the Army's Jupiter IRBM, which was to be turned over to the USAF.

The greatest success of the year came on December 17, the 24th anniversary of the Wright brothers' flight at Kitty Hawk. From the Cape Canaveral test center an Atlas blasted off its pad, flew 500 miles down range and impacted in a predefined target area, the first complete success for the big ICBM. The ballistic missiles were, of course, still in test status, but the road to their operational employment was now clearly marked.

*The Impact of Science and Technology*

Throughout a crucial period, continuing demand for improved performance in weapon systems dictated greater-than-ever concentration on research and development. Science also found its way into the non-combat segments of Air Force operations, in such areas as management, computerized supply systems and automated communications. And, in the latter years of the decade, there came the new dimension of space, one in which the military utility was nebulous but which nonetheless had to be explored as insurance against the future.

Never was the impact of science and technology so apparent as in the last two years of the fifties, when new systems came into being in so many areas that it is possible only to glossarize the major developments as symbols of a far broader program of Air Force advancement. Foremost, of course, was the ballistic missile. On February 28, 1958, the Department of Defense assigned responsibility for land-based ICBM's and IRBM's to the Air Force and at the same time directed the USAF to proceed with development of the solid-fuel, silo-sited Minuteman missile. The Thor IRBM joined operational units in 1959 and in June of that year the first Thor squadron was deployed to the United Kingdom. On September 1, 1959, the Atlas was added to SAC's inventory of deterrent systems and declared operational on September 9. By this time the Air Force's overall capability had been greatly strengthened by the introduction to service of many other types of missiles in the tactical and air defense categories.

As for airplanes, the B-52 was now available in large numbers, its utility soon to be enhanced by the Hound Dog missile, which could deliver a nuclear warhead 500 miles after launch from a late-model B-52. In December, 1958, the USAF awarded a contract to North American Aviation for development of a trisonic bomber, the XB-70. A fleet of Century Series fighters was in service and the Air Force, together with the Navy and NASA, was preparing to advance the frontier of aeronautical knowledge with the X-15, which was eventually to reach altitudes well above 50 miles and speeds of more than six times sound velocity.

In the new dimension of space, the Air Force was exploring the immediately apparent applications: weather, communications, navigation, surveillance and early warning. It was the Air Force which sent into orbit the first communications satellite, Project Score, on December 18, 1958. Two months later the USAF initiated a series of military/scientific satellites in Project Discoverer, which was to continue for several years and provide a wealth of space data. In 1958/59, the Air Force also started programs to investigate such other areas of space potential as inspection of unidentified satellites and man's utility in the space environment.

*Entering the Sixties*

On December 11, 1959, Dudley C. Sharp was sworn in as the sixth Secretary of the Air Force, succeeding James H. Douglas, Jr. Secretary Sharp brought to the post a broad background in business and government. He had, from October, 1955 until January, 1959, been Assistant Secretary of the Air Force for Materiel and for four months prior to his appointment as Secretary, he had served as Under Secretary.

Although the first ICBM had been declared operational, development in this area accelerated rather than slackened as the USAF sought to improve Atlas and bring Titan into early operational service. In March, 1960, the Air Force started a series of tests of an advanced Atlas employing the new inertial guidance system. Titan, meanwhile, was making its first flight tests at ranges of 5,000 miles and more.

The Air Force brought off a pair of dramatic space "firsts" in 1960. On August 11 it recovered the first man-made object from orbit, an 85-pound instrument capsule from Discoverer XIII. The capsule, ejected after 16 orbits, was tracked during its descent and recovered from the Pacific Ocean near Hawaii. The following week, on August 19, the USAF made the first mid-air recovery of an object from space, when the crew of a Fairchild C-119 transport snared a 300-pound capsule from Discoverer XIV.

The B-52 continued to demonstrate its long-distance prowess. On December 14, a B-52G completed a 10,000-mile nonstop flight without refueling, breaking several world records.

Air Force transport aircraft figured in international events during the year. When a series of earthquakes left millions homeless in Chile, the USAF flew 77 mercy missions, flying into the stricken area 877 tons of clothing, food and medical supplies, including two complete field hospitals. And when trouble broke out in the Congo, the USAF supported United Nations efforts to restore order by airlifting troops and supplies and evacuating civilians.

CONGO AIRLIFT AT KANO, NIGERIA, BY JOHN GROTH.

*Change of Command*

The Air Force experienced another dual change of leadership in the first half of 1961. In January, Eugene M. Zuckert became Secretary of the Air Force. No stranger to the USAF, Secretary Zuckert had been an Assistant Secretary in the late forties and early fifties and had also served as a member of the Atomic Energy Commission. On June 30, with the retirement of General White, the post of Chief of Staff went to General Curtis E. LeMay, wartime B-29 commander and prime mover in the massive build-up of Strategic Air Command during the fifties.

April saw a major organizational change. The Air Research and Development Command became the Air Force Systems Command with the assignment of handling advanced technology, testing and site activation and certain procurement, production and contract management responsibilities formerly held by Air Materiel Command. AMC, in turn, was reorganized as the Air Force Logistics Command, charged with maintenance, supply and other support of weapon systems and the procurement function for this responsibility.

In February, the USAF started tests of the solid-propellant Minuteman, designed for quick reaction in an emergency because it could be maintained "at the ready" in dispersed, underground silos, its solid propellants eliminating the time-consuming job of fueling before launch, a disadvantage of the earlier Atlas.

A major advance in air defense came with the introduction to operational service of the Bomarc pilotless interceptor. On June 1, the first Bomarc squadron was activated at Kincheloe AFB, Michigan, named for the Korean ace and X-2 pilot who had lost his life on a routine test flight in 1958.

During the year, the USAF formed the first Aerospace Surveillance and Control Squadron, part of the Space Detection and Tracking Systems of the North American Air Defense Command. An interim SPADATS control center was opened at Ent AFB, Colorado.

Also activated in 1961 was a bomb alarm system covering 14 areas of the United States and designed for extension to 97 potential target areas. The command and control system included an emergency automatic message transmission relay for contact between USAF headquarters and the commands, a mobile communication system for reaching key personnel in an emergency, and a Washington command post.

GENERAL CURTIS E. LeMAY, BY SANDOR KLEIN.

*Crisis in Cuba*

Important progress on many fronts was made by the Air Force in 1962. Beginning in April, Titan I squadrons joined SAC's operational missile force, and in December SAC received its first Minuteman solid-fueled, silo-launched missiles. Also in service was the last model of the Atlas, the ''F,'' which, like Minuteman, had silo-launching capability. Tests were started in mid-year of Titan II, a missile which used storable liquid fuels for rapid reaction in an emergency.

Two new airplanes were ordered into development: the McDonnell F-4C, a USAF tactical version of a Navy carrier-based fighter, and the trisonic, multipurpose General Dynamics F-111A, known initially as TFX.

The air defense mission was bolstered by the entry into operational service of two huge radar scanning stations of the Ballistic Missile Early Warning System; a third was being readied for use in 1963.

During the year, the National Aeronautics and Space Administration inaugurated orbital flights in its Project Mercury. The Air Force provided launch and recovery support for this program, and, by agreement with NASA, prepared to provide similar services for the follow-on Gemini program. The USAF continued with its own unmanned space research and progressed on its major space development, a high-energy booster named Titan III.

The Air Force established a Special Air Warfare Center at Eglin AFB, Florida, under Tactical Air Command. Mission of the center was to train U.S. and allied guerilla forces and develop weapon employment techniques for special air warfare. Many USAF personnel trained in guerilla tactics were assigned to Viet Nam as advisors to the Vietnamese Air Force and USAF transports were in use for training drops of South Vietnamese paratroops.

The outstanding event of the USAF year was the crisis in Cuba. On October 14, two Lockheed U-2 reconnaissance planes of the 4080th Strategic Wing discovered that Soviet missile sites were under construction in Cuba. President Kennedy immediately demanded that the USSR dismantle the sites and remove the missiles. In the tense period that followed, the USAF was extremely active. SAC's B-52's went on continuous airborne alert, insurance against escalation of the crisis, and the B-47's were flown to dispersal sites. Other SAC planes joined the Navy in maintaining a quarantine watch over shipping in the Atlantic. TAC's 19th Air Force established an advanced command post in Florida to exercise command over all tactical air units—USAF, Navy and Marine—in the potential combat zone. ADC shifted large numbers of its Convair F-102 and F-106 fighter-interceptors to Florida to fly patrols off the coast and reoriented a number of its radars to give warning of a Cuban-based missile attack. Both SAC and TAC flew continuous reconnaissance missions in the area until the Soviets had withdrawn the last of their missiles. Said Chief of Staff LeMay: ''Our aerospace power was being exercised throughout the world during the crisis, and awareness of the capability had its effect well beyond Cuba.''

ATLAS AT MISSILE SITE NUMBER EIGHT, BY
GERALD McCONNELL. *Beginning in 1962, USAF
ICBM's went underground, into hardened and
dispersed silos. Here an Atlas F is being removed
from its silo at Plattsburg AFB, New York, and
lowered to its trailer for transport to the maintenance shop.*

*A Manned Spacecraft Approved*

With hundreds of ICBM's in ready status and more being added every month, there was no longer a need for the overseas-based IRBM's. So, on January 11, the Air Force announced that the Thors based in England would be returned to the United States; Jupiter sites in Italy and Turkey were also to be dismantled. ICBM strength continued to mount as six squadrons equipped with Titan II became operational during the year. The USAF started the year with about 200 ICBM's emplaced; by the end of the year the number had reached 554.

In the aircraft field, the F-4C ordered the previous year made its initial flight on May 27, and on December 17, the huge Lockheed C-141 jet transport, capable of carrying more than 70,000 pounds of cargo, took to the air for the first time.

In June, the USAF turned over the last of its Pinetree radar sites to the Royal Canadian Air Force and in September the third of the BMEWS sites was activated at Flyingdales Moor, England.

By the end of 1963, launches of unmanned spacecraft in the intensive USAF science and applications program had stepped up to the rate of almost one a week. The Department of Defense directed a sudden change in the Air Force's efforts to explore the utility of man in space. The USAF had had under development a single-place winged spacecraft called Dyna-Soar, the prime purpose of which was exploration of controlled re-entry into the atmosphere. On December 10 Dyna-Soar was canceled and a new program—the Manned Orbiting Laboratory—initiated. The MOL was to be a long-duration spacecraft designed to investigate what military purposes man could serve in space and to check out new equipment and instrumentation. A long delay was to ensue before MOL entered hardware status in 1965; it was planned for operational use in 1968.

Late in 1963 the Air Force was an indirect participant in a dramatic and tragic episode of American history. When President Kennedy was assassinated in Dallas, President Lyndon B. Johnson was inaugurated in Air Force One, the Boeing VC-137 executive jet transport in which President Kennedy had flown to Texas.

*INAUGURATION IN AIR FORCE ONE, BY WALTER RICHARDS. President Lyndon B. Johnson was inaugurated in a USAF airplane, an executive jet known as Air Force One. In the painting, Judge Sarah T. Hughes administers the oath to the President, who is flanked on the left by Mrs. Johnson and Representative Albert Thomas and on the right by Mrs. Jacqueline Kennedy and Representative Jack Brooks.*

*Trisonic Aircraft*

While the ICBM build-up continued in 1964, the Air Force was controverting the oft-repeated opinion that the manned military airplane was "dead" with a series of developments on the aeronautical front.

In February, the USAF announced activation of two wings of McDonnell F-4C high performance fighters and in October the reconnaissance version of the plane was added to the TAC inventory. The advent of the F-4C was marked by a demonstration of its capability on December 1–2; four F-4C's of the 12th Tactical Fighter Wing set an endurance record by flying almost 10,000 miles on an 18-hour nonstop flight.

But even greater fighter performance was in the offing. In February, President Johnson announced the existence of a 2,000 mile-per-hour fighter, the Lockheed YF-12A, and on December 22 a sister plane, the SR-71 long-range strategic reconnaissance aircraft, made its first flight. A day earlier, the trisonic F-111A had gone aloft for the first time.

Meanwhile, in September, the 2,000 mile-per-hour XB-70A superbomber had started its flight test program. The XB-70A was doomed to remain an experimental airplane, but, even before its first flight, the USAF submitted a proposal to the Department of Defense for a new Advanced Manned Strategic Aircraft.

On July 2, the first of 17 new Boeing KC-135B flying command posts was delivered to SAC and in the same week SAC's Command and Control System began operational testing.

In October, Military Air Transport Service received its first deliveries of the Lockheed C-141 jet troop carrier/cargo airplane. Late in the year the USAF received approval to develop a gigantic supertransport, the C-5A, which would have three times the cargo capacity of the C-141.

In space research, the Air Force progressed with the start of flight tests of its Titan III booster and the initial tests of a 156-inch diameter solid-fuel rocket motor, the largest ever fired.

As the new year started, the Air Force bade farewell to one of its greatest leaders. On February 1 General LeMay retired after 35 years of commissioned service.

GENERAL CURTIS E. LeMAY WITH PT-1, DURING HIS RETIRE-
MENT CEREMONY, BY WOODI ISHMAEL. The PT-1 became the
standard primary trainer in 1927, when the ''Jenny'' was retired
from service.

*Action in Viet-Nam*

General LeMay was succeeded by his Vice Chief of Staff for the previous six months, General John P. McConnell, who had come to USAF headquarters from a tour as Deputy Commander-in-Chief of the joint European Command.

In 1965, the Air Force was engaged in a new war, one which bore many resemblances to the Korean action. In the face of continued aggressive moves by the Communists, President Johnson directed the bombardment of military targets in North Viet Nam. Stating that he regretted the necessity for such measures, the President listed the ''whys'': ''We destroy bridges so it is harder to convey the instruments of war from North to South. We destroy radar stations to keep our planes from being shot down. We destroy military depots for the infiltration of men and arms to the South. We patrol routes of communications to halt the invaders. We destroy ammunition dumps to prevent the use of explosives against our men and our allies. . . . However, the bombing is not an end in itself. Its purpose is to bring us closer to peace.''

The Air Force was performing effectively in carrying out the President's order. USAF fighters, fighter-bombers and even B-52's flying from Guam were delivering destruction to the enemy. Other aircraft were escorting helicopters, transports, convoys, trains and boats. Still others were flying close support for ground troops and four squadrons of assault transports were providing airlift for both United States and South Vietnamese forces.

At home, the Air Force continued to advance its overall capability. Indicative of the emphasis on scientific and technological development in the modern USAF was the appointment of Dr. Harold Brown, noted scientist and Director of Defense Research and Engineering since May, 1961, as Secretary of the Air Force. Having served the longest tenure of any Secretary, Eugene M. Zuckert retired on September 30, 1965.

Earlier, the last of 800 Minuteman I ICBM's had been emplaced. The older Atlases and Titans were being withdrawn from service and the new, improved Minuteman II was coming into being as the USAF moved toward its goal of 1,000 operational ICBM's. Modern aircraft were flowing into service units and the USAF space program was accelerating. The Air Force had come a long way from the first military airplane trials of 1908.

GENERAL JOHN P. McCONNELL, BY WOODI ISHMAEL.

# CHAPTER VI

# The Global Air Force

*The Modern Air Force*

From its headquarters in the Pentagon, the United States Air Force operates a global command with manifold responsibilities; they can be summarized as the maintenance of ''general aerospace supremacy.''

More specifically, the USAF has the major functions of supporting the national policy of deterring aggression, defending the United States against air attack, controlling vital aerospace areas; also, conducting strategic and tactical warfare against the enemy if deterrence fails, furnishing tactical air support for the ground forces, and providing logistics support, such as airlift and resupply of airborne operations. Other tasks include conducting strategic and tactical reconnaissance and meteorological study, meeting the major space research requirements of the Department of Defense and, additionally, providing support to the programs of the National Aeronautics and Space Administration through research and development of spacecraft, launch vehicles and other space exploration equipment.

The general assignment of ''support'' involves such missions as airlift and resupply of Army units, aeromedical evacuation, rescue services for disasters anywhere in the free world, recovery service for astronauts, weather fore-casting, and surveys leading to continual upgrading of maps and charts for all uses. The USAF also trains forces to help the Navy in interdiction of enemy sea power, antisubmarine warfare and aerial mine-laying operations.

The USAF's primary weapon systems are aircraft and missiles, some of them with nuclear capability, others non-nuclear, and still others with the flexibility to handle either type. Missiles range from the long-range ICBM's to small air-to-air rockets carried by interceptor aircraft. A great many different types of aircraft are employed to perform specific assignments; in all, the USAF operates about 15,000 planes and there are an additional 2,500 in the Air Reserve Forces.

There are more than one and a half million people in the Air Force. The active duty complement of officers and airmen totals about 850,000 and the USAF employs some 325,000 civilians. There are, in addition, more than 430,000 members of the Air Force Reserve and the Air National Guard.

The Air Force is organized into a number of major commands and separate agencies, each with specific missions in maintaining the peace or winning a war. Its area of interest, stretching from the North Polar regions to Antarctica and touching on all the continents, makes it truly a global air force.

PRE-DAWN AIR FORCE MISSILE TEST, BY TRAN MAWICKE.

*Air Defense Command*

Charged with the responsibility for training, equipping and operating USAF forces required for the aerospace defense of North America (excluding Alaska), Air Defense Command is the Air Force element of the North American Air Defense Command. The headquarters is located at Ent Air Force Base, Colorado.

Five of ADC's seven air divisions control interceptor operations: the 25th Air Division, headquartered at McChord AFB, Washington; the 26th Air Division at Stewart AFB, New York; the 28th Air Division at Hamilton AFB, California; the 29th Air Division at Richards-Gebaur AFB, Missouri; and the 30th Air Division at Truax Field, Wisconsin. The 73rd Air Division, Tyndall AFB, Florida, operates the ADC Weapons Center and conducts crew training. The 9th Air Division at Colorado Springs operates the Ballistic Missile Early Warning System (BMEWS) and the Spacetrack System, a network of radar and optical equipment which tracks objects in space and relays tracking data to NORAD's Space Detection and Tracking System.

For its surveillance mission, ADC has some 200 radar stations, most of them tied into the SAGE (Semi-Automatic Ground Environment) system. SAGE is a warning and control system in which information from the radars is fed into digital computers through a communications network. The computers plot courses for interception of unidentified aircraft and simultaneously control all air defense weapons.

ADC has two BMEWS sites—Clear, Alaska, and Thule, Greenland. A third site, at Flyingdales Moor, England, is jointly operated by ADC and the Royal Air Force. ADC also has responsibility for operation of the Distant Early Warning line along the Arctic Circle.

Supplementing the land-based radars and extending detection range seaward, the command has two wings of airborne early warning and control aircraft, one at Otis AFB, Massachusetts, the other at McClellan AFB, California. For surveillance of southern coastal waters, a squadron from one wing is based at McCoy AFB, Florida.

ADC fighter-interceptor squadrons are equipped with four types of high performance aircraft. The long-range McDonnell F-101B and the Convair F-106 fire Falcon missiles and Genie nuclear rockets. The Convair F-102A is armed with Falcons and the Lockheed F-104A carries Sidewinder missiles and the Vulcan 20 millimeter cannon. Complementary to the manned aircraft are six operational sites equipped with the Bomarc B surface-to-air missile, which flies at more than twice the speed of sound and which carries a nuclear warhead to destroy invading aircraft within a range of 400 miles.

ALERT ROOM BETWEEN BOGEYS, BY CARL
SETTERBERG. A chess game at ADC's Hamilton
AFB.

ALONG THE COAST NEAR SEATTLE, BY ART RILEY.

*THE CROSS AND THE SWORD, BY BOB POOLE. In this scene at Thule, Greenland, where ADC operates a BMEWS site, the artist expresses the thought that both the church and the Air Force are symbols of strength and protection.*

*Air Force Logistics Command*

The job of the Air Force Logistics Command is to keep the USAF's weapon systems ready for action, to provide the logistics support the combat commands need to maintain their aircraft, missiles and other equipment at top efficiency. Headquartered at Wright-Patterson AFB, Ohio, AFLC has four main functions: procurement, supply, maintenance and transportation. Procurement involves primarily the purchasing of spare parts and aerospace ground equipment and letting contracts for technical services. Supply is the management of some 1,800,000 different items in the inventory, cataloging, stocking and funneling them to the bases where they are needed. About 100,000 persons are engaged in the modification and overhaul of USAF materiel. AFLC provides management and planning for transportation support of manned aircraft, missiles and space systems and controls LOGAIR, the Air Force contract airlift for the movement of high-value and priority cargo from warehouse to user.

Among the specialized organizations within AFLC is the Ground Electronics Engineering Installation Agency, which manages the engineering, installation and maintenance of all USAF ground communications and electronic equipment—radar, radio, teletype and telephones. The 2802nd Inertial Guidance and Calibration Group at Newark Air Force Station, Ohio, repairs and maintains the accuracy of the guidance systems in the USAF's long-range missiles and the navigation systems in certain new, advanced aircraft. At Davis-Monthan AFB, Arizona, there is the 2704th Air Force Aircraft Storage and Disposition Group, the USAF's ''parts bank,'' which monitors surplus property, salvages and disposes of equipment ranging from obsolete planes to books.

The industrial-type units which carry out most of AFLC's operational functions are the Air Material Areas, some of which employ more than 20,000 persons. Each AMA is assigned a group of weapons or support systems for which it provides world-wide logistics management. The Oklahoma City AMA, for instance, repairs and furnishes spare parts for the Boeing B-52 and B-47 bombers, their tankers, certain other aircraft, air-to-surface missiles and a number of ground communications and electronics systems. There are nine AMA's, the others located at Middletown, Pennsylvania; San Bernardino, California; Ogden, Utah; Mobile, Alabama; San Antonio, Texas; Sacramento, California; Rome, New York; and Robins AFB, Georgia.

*JET ENGINE REPAIRS, BY DAVID KLEIN.*

Research and development for the advancement of aerospace technology and for equipping the Air Force of tomorrow with superior weapons and equipment are the responsibilities of the Air Force Systems Command, which has its headquarters at Andrews AFB, Maryland. AFSC carries out extensive research programs in its own facilities and supervises the activities of aerospace manufacturers developing aircraft, missiles, spacecraft, launch vehicles and associated equipment under contract to the Air Force. The command directs the expenditure of some 40 percent of the annual Air Force budget. A far-flung organization, it manages about 300 installations in the United States, England, South Africa, Greenland, Eniwetok and Singapore. Major units within the command include nine divisions and five test and development centers.

Two of the divisions are located at the sprawling Air Force complex in Ohio, Wright-Patterson AFB: the Aeronautical Systems Division, which manages the development and procurement of USAF aircraft and aeronautical equipment; and the Foreign Technology Division, which collects, evaluates and passes on to the other commands information about foreign aerospace progress. The Electronic Systems Division, Hanscom Field, Massachusetts manages developmental programs in such areas as communications command, control, warning, surveillance, intelligence and weather systems. Headquartered at Bolling AFB, Washington, D.C., is the Research and Technology Division, which has a number of laboratories engaged in specific areas of research. The Air Force Weapons Laboratory at Kirtland AFB, N.M. conducts research in nuclear weapons applications. The Rome Air Development Center, Griffiss AFB, New York has a wide variety of responsibilities, providing research and development support for programs in ground communications hardware, intelligence devices, air navigation and electromagnetic radiation warfare, to name just a few areas of its interest. At Edwards AFB, California, there is the Air Force Rocket Propulsion Laboratory, which is involved in research on rocket engines and components, propellants and associated ground equipment. The Research and Technology Division has four other laboratories at Wright-Patterson AFB, the nature of whose research effort is contained in their titles: Aero-Propulsion Laboratory, Materials Laboratory, Flight Dynamics Laboratory and Avionics (aviation electronics) Laboratory.

Based in Los Angeles, California, is AFSC's Contract Management Division, which monitors the work of defense plants for which the USAF has cognizance. (*Continued*)

*TEST PILOT, BY STAN GALLI. In the expressive face of his subject, artist Galli captures the courage, determination and spirit of the men of Systems Command who vie with the unknown*

ARMING AN F-105 AT EGLIN AFB, BY DEAN ELLIS.

*VANDENBERG AFB, BY JOE CLEARY. The missile ready for test represents the type of missile and space development work being carried out at the Western Test Range.*

*BLAST OFF, BY FRANK GERMAIN.*

BIG ANNIE ON THE PAD, BY SI MEZEROW.

*Air Force Systems Command (Continued)*

AFSC has three divisions which focus their effort on missiles and spacecraft. At Andrews AFB, home of the parent command, is the National Range Division, which operates two test ranges in support of the national intercontinental ballistic missile and space programs: the Air Force Eastern Test Range at Patrick AFB, Florida, and the Air Force Western Test Range at Vandenberg AFB, California.

The Space Systems Division, Los Angeles, California plans and manages programs for research, development and acquisition of space equipment and the Ballistic Missile Division, Norton AFB, California, has similar responsibilities in the field of ballistic missilery.

Medical research in support of development of new Air Force aircraft and spacecraft is conducted by the Aerospace Medical Division at Brooks AFB, Texas. The division's units include the USAF School of Aviation Medicine, located at Brooks AFB, and six laboratories at other bases.

Best known of Systems Command's centers is the Air Force Flight Test Center at Edwards AFB, California, where the primary activity is the testing of new aircraft to insure that they meet USAF requirements. The center is also the home of the USAF Aerospace Research Pilot School, where military astronauts are trained. Another unit of the center is the USAF Parachute Test Group at El Centro, California.

At Kirtland AFB, New Mexico, there is the Air Force Special Weapons Center. The ''special weapons'' for which the center provides test facilities and engineering support are those of the nuclear and thermonuclear variety.

The Air Proving Ground Center, Eglin AFB, Florida, conducts development engineering tests of complete aircraft and missiles and their equipment, for which it operates the Gulf Test Range.

The Air Force Missile Development Center, Holloman AFB, New Mexico, concentrates its research effort on particular types of missiles other than the ICBM's, for instance, air-to-air weapons and drone aircraft. It also operates an inertial guidance test facility and conducts rocket firings in a research program on re-entry technology.

Finally, at Arnold Air Force Station, Tennessee, there is the largest complex of wind tunnels, high-altitude test cells and simulation chambers in the free world: Arnold Engineering Development Center. AEDC provides test support in the fields of gas dynamics and propulsion for all the military services, the National Aeronautics and Space Administration, industrial contractors, colleges and universities and independent research organizations.

IN THE HAND OF GOD, BY BARYE PHILLIPS.

MID-AIR CAPTURE OF DISCOVERER XIV, BY REN WICKS. As part of its new responsibility for exploring the military potential of space, the Air Force developed a technique whereby objects are recovered after orbiting by ''snatch'' aircraft like this C-119 of the 6593rd Air Recovery Group.

*CAPSULE RECOVERY, BY REN WICKS. After the mid-air catch, crewmen haul the space capsule into the C-119. The scene depicted here was the recovery of Discoverer XIV, ejected from space by earth signal after 17 orbits and "snatched" at an altitude of 8,500 feet as it descended through the atmosphere. It was the first mid-air recovery in history, made on August 19, 1960.*

*Air Training Command*

Take a young American and train him to become a skilled airman, technician or manager for the Air Force—that is the assignment of the Air Training Command, headquartered at Randolph AFB, Texas. ATC operates 18 bases in the United States and some 200 field and mobile training detachments around the world. Its mission involves recruiting and military, technical and flying training.

The USAF Recruiting Service, also at Randolph AFB, enlists about 100,000 men a year, conducting, in the process, interviews of more than a million persons.

Military training consists of introducing new enlistees to the Air Force way of life and assigning them to further training according to the needs of the USAF. The course involves six weeks of basic training at the Lackland Military Training Center, Lackland AFB, Texas. Also at Lackland AFB is the Officer Training School, which provides an intensive three-month program for college graduates, and special schools for chaplains and law school graduates entering the Air Force.

The command operates seven centers responsible for primary and advanced technical training of most non-rated specialists. The centers are located at Keesler (Mississippi), Sheppard (Texas), Chanute (Illinois), Lowry (Colorado), Amarillo (Texas) Air Force Bases and at Lackland AFB. More than 100,000 officers and airmen are graduated annually from one or more of the 700 courses conducted by the centers. A sampling of the courses includes such diversified subjects as air traffic control, missile guidance systems, aircraft mechanics, missiles and space boosters, armament, intelligence, firefighting, weather observation, airframe repair, metal working, personnel administration, supply, cryptography and handling of sentry dogs.

ATC has 12 bases engaged in flying training, eight of them conducting undergraduate pilot training, the other providing aircrew training. Aircraft used in the program include: the single-engine, propeller-driven Cessna T-41A; the Cessna T-37 primary jet trainer; the Lockheed T-33 advanced jet trainer; the Northrop T-38 supersonic trainer; the Convair T-29 "flying classroom," which carries 14 student navigators and two instructors; and the North American T-39 used, along with the T-33 and T-38, in the pilot instructor courses. Undergraduate pilot trainees receive 30 hours of instruction in the T-41A, 90 hours in the T-37 and 120 hours in the T-38. Undergraduate navigator training is conducted at James Connally AFB, Texas, advanced navigator-bombardier and electronic warfare officer courses at Mather AFB, California. ATC had a specialized installation at Stead AFB, Nevada, where the primary mission was training in survival, escape and evasion. Helicopter training was also conducted at Stead AFB, pending its deactivation.

*THE AIR FORCE FLYING CADET, BY ROBERT HANDVILLE.*
*Preparing tomorrow's flying officers for their Air Force careers is*
*one of the prime responsibilities of Air Training Command.*

*A WINNER AT LACKLAND, BY BOB POOLE.*

*T-38's ON FINAL TURN, BY KEITH FERRIS.*

*Air University and Air Force Academy*

The Air University is the Air Force's educational center for career officers. Its job is to produce air commanders and staff officers in much the same way as a civilian medical school trains doctors for their practice. The Air University has its headquarters and its major schools at Maxwell AFB, Alabama. Other schools are located at Gunter AFB, Alabama, and Wright-Patterson AFB, Ohio.

There are three rungs on the AU's advanced educational ladder. The lower is for junior officers—lieutenants and captains—of the USAF and the flying forces of other nations, who are given a 14-week course of lectures and seminars at the Squadron Officer School. Next rung is the Air Command and Staff College, which offers a nine-month course designed to prepare field grade officers for upper level assignments. At the top of the ladder is the Air War College which readies senior officers for high command posts. The Air University also offers a number of specialized courses, including correspondence training, at four schools and administers the Air Force Reserve Officers Training Corps.

The mission of the United States Air Force Academy is to provide instruction and experience to cadets to qualify them as career Air Force officers. Located at Colorado Springs, Colorado, the Academy provides a four-year, college-type course in academic subjects and parallel instruction in military professionalism. Among the professional subjects are the tactical and strategic use of weapon systems, weapons and techniques of the past, present and future, and defense planning and operations. The academic curriculum is neither an engineering nor a liberal arts program, but it combines certain elements of both. In both the professional and academic courses, the aim is not to train cadets for specific jobs, but to give them a foundation for Air Force career fields they may enter after graduation.

Upon completion of the course, the cadet is commissioned a second lieutenant in the USAF and is graduated with a bachelor of science degree. Under a cooperative program with civilian universities, certain cadets are selected for post-graduate study at the civilian institutions, where they may earn master's degrees within seven months after their graduation from the Academy.

## Military Air Transport Service

Known primarily as a transportation command, the Military Air Transport Service actually has a much broader mission which includes rescue, weather, photographic and geodetic services for the Department of Defense. Headquarters of MATS, which becomes Military Airlift Command on January 1, 1966, is at Scott AFB, Illinois.

The global airlift function is handled by two sub-commands: Eastern Transport Air Force at McGuire AFB, New Jersey, and Western Transport Air Force, Travis AFB, California. EASTAF covers the world from the Mississippi eastward to Calcutta, India,—WESTAF the remainder.

Slightly more than half of MATS' airlift operation is in the "special mission" category, including mobility training exercises, movement of intercontinental missiles and other outsize cargo, transporting equipment to Southeast Asia and humanitarian lift, such as delivery of food to famine-stricken areas. The other part of the airlift assignment involves regular operations over some 115,000 miles of established routes all over the world. Two specialized airlift units include the 1254th Air Transport Wing, Andrews AFB, Maryland, which provides transportation for high-level United States and foreign dignitaries, and the 1707th Air Transport Wing, Tinker AFB, Oklahoma, which operates MATS' graduate training school.

MATS' technical service organizations include: Air Weather Service, Scott AFB, which operates a world-wide weather observation and forecasting network at 400 locations and also conducts advanced weather research; Air Rescue Service, Orlando AFB, Florida, which provides search and rescue coverage and additionally handles the recovery mission for space flights; and the Air Photographic and Charting Service, also at Orlando, which provides the Air Force and in some cases other elements of the Department of Defense with geodetic and photographic services.

MATS also administers the Civil Reserve Air Fleet—some 350 passenger and cargo airplanes owned by 22 commercial airlines—which would augment existing forces in an emergency, and more than 250 transport units of the Air Reserve Forces.

MATS aircraft include the fan-jet powered Lockheed C-141; the turbojet Boeing C-135; the turboprop Lockheed C-130; and the propeller driven Douglas C-118, C-124 and C-133 transports. The 1254th ATW operates, in addition, about 30 planes, including the Boeing VC-137, a military version of the 707 commercial jetliner, and the Lockheed VC-140, a smaller, shorter-range jet.

*HICKAM AFB WAITING ROOM, BY THORNTON UTZ.*

*STOP-OVER AT BELUM FIELD, NEW DELHI, INDIA, BY THORNTON UTZ.*

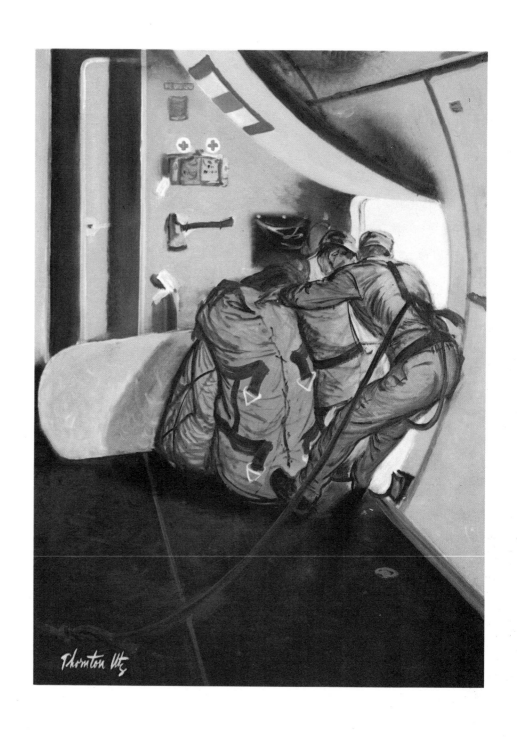

MATS AIR-SEA RESCUE OPERATION, BY THORNTON UTZ.

*MIDNIGHT SUN, BY AL MUENCHEN. The C-130E flying over Tucker Glacier in Antarctica exemplifies the global nature of MATS operation.*

*Strategic Air Command*

The mission of the Strategic Air Command is to prevent war, to deter an aggressor from launching a strike against the United States or other free world nations by maintaining a massive nuclear and thermonuclear retaliatory capability.

SAC headquarters is at Offutt AFB, Nebraska. In wartime, the SAC commander would direct his force from an underground command post at the headquarters base. Should the headquarters be destroyed, continuity of command is assured by use of an airborne command post containing a controller team directed by a general officer. The airborne post, a specially-equipped EC-135 jet, is a complete command and communications center which can maintain contact with all SAC installations.

SAC has four numbered air forces: The Second Air Force, Barksdale AFB, Louisiana; the Eighth at Westover AFB, Massachusetts; the Fifteenth, March AFB, California; and the Sixteenth, Terrejon AFB, Spain. There are also the 3rd Air Division in Guam and the 1st Strategic Aerospace Division at Vandenberg AFB, California.

SAC has operated a mixed weapons force since September 9, 1959, when a SAC crew fired its first Atlas ICBM. There are now some 850 ICBM's in operational status, most of them the solid-fueled, silo-launched Minuteman. Remainder of the missile force includes Titan II and Atlas F weapons, also fired from silos.

In addition to the ICBM's, SAC operates more than 1,600 combat aircraft. Mainstay of the fleet is the Boeing B-52 Stratofortress, about 650 of which are in service. There are also 80 supersonic Convair B-58's and more than 200 Boeing B-47 medium bombers. For range extension of the bombers, SAC employs a tanker fleet of some 600 jet-powered Boeing KC-135's and propeller-driven Boeing KC-97's.

Twenty-nine of the B-52 wings are equipped with the Hound Dog air-to-surface missile, carried under the wing of the bomber and capable of striking a target 500 miles from launch point, making the B-52's mobile missile platforms. Part of the B-52 force is always in the air on airborne alert, remaining aloft as long as 24 hours by means of the in-flight refueling technique.

The combined force of ICBM's and bombers give SAC the most powerful strike force in history.

*B-52's AROUND THE EARTH, BY ALEXANDER KORTNER. The artist expresses the world-ranging capability of SAC's bombers.*

*TWIN B-52 ENGINES, BY DONALD CROWLEY.*

*B-52 OVER THE NORTH ATLANTIC, BY RALPH ILIGAN.*

*THE FIRST MINUTEMAN, BY CHET COLLOM. The scene depicts the installation of the first silo-launched Minuteman ICBM at Malmstrom AFB in 1962. The sentry dog, like Minuteman, is symbolic of guardianship of the nation.*

*Tactical Air Command*

Equipped to fight large or small wars with nuclear or conventional weapons, Tactical Air Command is the Air Force's long-range, mobile strike force. The command operates on a global basis, either independently or in conjunction with other air or surface forces. Its major assignments include tactical fighter operations, tactical reconnaissance, assault airlift and "Special Air Warfare." TAC has headquarters at Langley AFB, Virginia.

Special Air Warfare involves development of tactics and equipment for counterinsurgency, unconventional and psychological operations. For this purpose, TAC maintains the USAF Special Air Warfare Center at Eglin AFB, Florida.

TAC's primary organization consists of three air forces: the Nineteenth Air Force at Seymour Johnson AFB, North Carolina; the Ninth, Shaw AFB, South Carolina; and the Twelfth, Waco, Texas.

Both a combat and a support command, TAC provides the U.S. Strike Command with its air component for rapid response to emergency situations anywhere in the world. The command also has responsibility for tactical air planning for the Middle East, certain parts of Africa and southern Asia. In support of air forces in Europe and the Pacific, TAC provides fighter and assault airlift squadrons and crews for tactical missile squadrons on a rotational basis. TAC is also responsible for logistic support in southern Asia.

In war, TAC would augment overseas tactical air forces and participate in Western Hemisphere defense by strengthening the Air Defense Command, providing fighters' and assault airlift units for the defense of Canada, the Caribbean and the United States, conduct reconnaissance operations to assess bomb damage in those areas, and airlift Army forces to critical areas.

In addition to the Special Air Warfare Center, TAC maintains two other specialized centers: the USAF Tactical Reconnaissance Center at Shaw AFB and the USAF Tactical Air Warfare Center at Eglin AFB. Schools include the USAF Tactical Missile School, Orlando AFB, Florida (where TAC trains crews in the operation of the Mace missile) and the USAF Air Ground Operations School at Eglin AFB.

Primary aircraft include the Republic F-105 fighter-bomber, the two-place McDonnell F-4C fighter and RF-4C recon version, and the Lockheed C-130E assault airlift transport. TAC uses SAC's Boeing KC-135 tanker fleet for in-flight refueling. Coming into the inventory soon is the high-performance General Dynamics F-111A.

198

*THUNDERBIRDS TAKE OFF AT NELLIS AIR FORCE BASE, BY KEITH FERRIS. The Thunderbirds are Tactical Air Command's demonstration team.*

*THROUGH DESERT JUNIPER, BY ART RILEY. The artist expresses the "toughness" of the USAF flyer through the picturesque juniper, one of the few trees tough enough to survive the hot, dry weather of the California desert.*

*A COLUMN OF BIRDS, BY WESLEY McKEOWN.*

CLIMBING ABOARD, BY HARRY SHAARE.

*OPERATION DESERT STRIKE, BY SAM McKIM.*
*TAC aircraft provide close support in an air-*
*ground exercise in California.*

THE ''SCREAMING EAGLES'' EMBARK ON A
C-130, BY MARBURY BROWN. Rapid movement
of troops to combat zones is a major TAC assignment.

IRANIAN PARATROOPS JUMPING FROM U.S.-MADE C-130, BY
MARBURY BROWN. Another TAC responsibility is provision of
training assistance to friendly nations.

*Alaskan Air Command*

The air component of the unified United States Alaskan Command, the Alaskan Air Command has multiple responsibilities: early warning of attack on the North American continent, air defense of Alaska, support of Strategic Air Command in Alaska, and support of special projects assigned either by the Air Force or USAC. Command headquarters is located at Elmendorf AFB, near Anchorage.

The warning mission is accomplished by two radar networks, the outer band being the Alaskan segment of the Distant Early Warning line extending along the Arctic Ocean, the inner a chain of ground-controlled intercept radars. The data collected from these latter stations is evaluated by four master direction centers and passed on to the North American Air Defense Command. Military personnel of the command man all the aircraft control and warning sites and the DEW line stations in the Aleutians; the Alaskan segment of the northern DEW line is operated by civilians under contract with Air Defense Command.

To overcome the problems of highly unreliable communications in the Arctic and sub-Arctic regions, the command operates a unique system known as "White Alice." White Alice is a radio relay system using over-the-horizon transmission known as "forward propagation tropospheric scatter"; its ultra high frequency beams carry for 200 miles on a single relay. AAC also has a military long distance dialing system which permits site commanders to telephone directly to headquarters.

Because of the weather and terrain, logistics support in Alaska is difficult; outlying stations have to be supplied almost entirely by air. For this purpose, AAC operates a fleet of Lockheed C-130 and Fairchild C-123 transports which deliver about 250 tons a day.

For support of SAC operations, AAC provides launching platforms, air defense and general housekeeping at Elmendorf and Eielson AFB's.

Elmendorf AFB is the home base for the command's all-weather interceptors, with elements operating from three forward bases including Eielson AFB. The interceptors are Convair F-102's and F-106's.

*ESKIMO VILLAGE, KOTZEBUE, ALASKA, BY LLOYD HARTING.*

*Pacific Air Forces*

Headquartered at Hickam AFB, Hawaii, Pacific Air Forces is the USAF's tactical aerospace arm in the central and western Pacific, the Far East and southeast Asia. It also doubles as the air component of the unified United States Pacific Command.

PACAF's missions in a general war are to conduct offensive operations designed to reduce an enemy's capability of attack and to wage defensive air warfare to protect the land areas of the Pacific Command and the western approaches to the United States. PACAF's tactical units would also perform such missions as air/ground operations, reconnaissance and airlift, teaming with other U.S. forces and those of the nation's partners in Pacific defense.

PACAF has five major subordinate elements. Most of the command's offensive, defensive and reconnaissance force comes under the Fifth Air Force at Fuchu Air Station, Japan. At Clark Air Base in the Philippines, the Thirteenth Air Force maintains units for operations in the Philippines, Marianas, Taiwan and southeast Asia. The Air Force role in Viet Nam is carried out by the Thirteenth's 2nd Air Division at Saigon. Intra-theater airlift and assault capability for all Pacific Command forces is provided by the 315th Air Division based in Japan. Responsibility for air defense of the Hawaiian Islands is assigned to the 326th Air Division, headquartered at Wheeler AFB, Hawaii. Also in Hawaii is the PACAF Base Command, which provides support for PACAF bases and operations of other commands, such as SAC, TAC and MATS.

In addition to the PACAF capability, there are more than 70 tactical squadrons belonging to free Eastern nations, allied with the United States by formal agreements such as the Southeast Asia Treaty Organization and the Australia-New Zealand-United States Alliance. PACAF participates in large-scale annual military exercises with SEATO forces and lesser scale joint maneuvers with other groups of allies.

In addition, PACAF conducts a continuous program of cooperative training of the air forces of these nations under the Military Assistance Program. The aim is to develop a higher degree of operational standardization and a closer alignment of procedures among the many nations to produce a strong, combined tactical air force in the East.

GUAMANIAN CHILDREN, BY ROY BESSER.

CONSTRUCTION WORKERS AT AN AIR BASE IN THAILAND, BY JAMES BAMA.

*C-130 AT INDIA/CHINA BORDER, BY BARYE PHILLIPS.*

SETTING UP AN AIR BASE AT TAOYUAN, FORMOSA, BY EARL GROSS.

*USAF FRIENDS NEAR K-9, KOREA, BY GEORGE C. BALES.*

*BAGUIO ROAD, THE PHILIPPINES, BY NOEL QUINN.*

*UP THE CREEK ON BLUE MONDAY (THE PHILIPPINES), BY BILL BENDER.*

GUARDIANS, BY CHARLES J. KUDERNA. Artist Kuderna sees the USAF in the Orient as a guardian of an old and mysterious culture, a role depicted by the flight of F-102's on patrol before an Okinawan ceremonial dancer.

*BEACH AT NAHA CITY, OKINAWA, BY REYNOLD BROWN.*

*THUNDER OVER OKINAWA, BY NIXON GALLOWAY.*

*ENTRANCE TO CAVES AND UNDERGROUND SHRINE, NAHA, OKINAWA, BY REYNOLD BROWN.*

*A DAY AT KAMAKURA (JAPAN), BY AL DEMPSTER.*

*ON THE INLAND SEA (JAPAN), BY AL DEMPSTER.*

*SENTINELS (JAPAN), BY COLLIN CAMPBELL.*

THUNDER AT DAWN, BY COLLIN CAMPBELL.

*PLANE AND GUIDE, BY BOB GREENBERG.*

ORPHANAGE AT MAYAHANA, BY AL BUELL.

*United States Air Forces in Europe*

The complex mission of the United States Air Forces in Europe, stated in simplest terms, is maintenance of a combat-ready force for possible defense of the West. USAFE has an area of responsibility covering some 600,000,000 square miles. It extends from the British Isles and Scandinavia through western Europe to North Africa, the Middle East and into Asia as far as Pakistan. The command provides support for several hundred installations in a dozen countries.

With headquarters at Lindsey Air Station, Wiesbaden, Germany, USAFE is, on the one hand, responsible to the Air Force Chief of Staff in matters of policy and command, and on the other, to the Commander in Chief, United States European Command. USAFE's principal operational commands are the Third Air Force, headquartered at South Ruislip, England, and the Seventeenth Air Force at Ramstein AB, Germany. A third major subcommand is the United States Logistics Group at Ankara, Turkey, which supports U.S. forces in Turkey, Greece and Crete and other areas in Africa, the Middle East and Asia. Also under USAFE is the 322nd Air Division (MATS), based at Chateauroux, France, which is the single agency for management of airlift in the European Theater.

USAFE aircraft earmarked for wartime use by the North Atlantic Treaty Organization include six tactical wings, two tactical reconnaissance wings and a tactical missile wing, the largest single air contribution of any nation in the 15-country alliance. USAFE units of the Third and Seventeenth Air Forces would be assigned to the 4th Allied Tactical Air Force, also at Ramstein. In addition, USAFE controls tactical rotational squadrons which would have NATO assignments with the 5th ATAF, Vicenza, Italy, and the 6th ATAF, Izmir, Turkey. One USAFE fighter-interceptor squadron under control of the Royal Netherlands Air Force would be assigned to the 2nd ATAF, Moenchen-Gladbach, Germany.

The USAFE aircraft inventory totals about 1,000 aircraft of a variety of types: the veteran North American F-100, the McDonnell F-101 and the Republic F-105 fighters. For reconnaissance, USAFE has the RF-101, operating from bases in France and Germany, and the Douglas RB-66, flying from bases in France and England. The air defense mission is performed by the Convair F-102 interceptor. For airlift, USAFE operates Lockheed C-130 and Douglas C-124 transports. The command is also equipped with two versions of the Martin Mace tactical missile.

*WATCH ON THE RHINE, BY ROBERT GEISSMAN.*

*CHAPEL AT NEUBIBERG AFB, GERMANY, BY JOHN PIKE.*

TEMPLE OF POSEIDON (GREECE), BY RAY PROHASKA.

*THE SPECTATORS, BY BARYE PHILLIPS. The painting shows the loading at Wheelus AFB, Tripoli, of United Nations troops for service in the Congo as a group of Moslem natives watch with interest.*

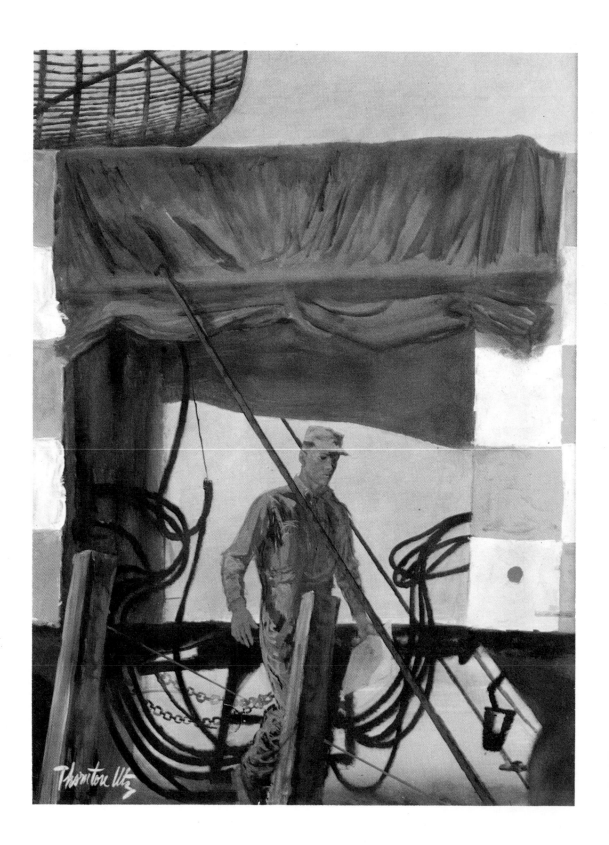

234

ARABS AND A C-119 AT WHEELUS AFB, TRIPOLI, BY ROBERT HANDVILLE.

*United States Air Forces Southern Command*

The United States Air Forces Southern Command is charged with planning and conduct of operations as directed by the commander of the United States Southern Command, of which it is the air component. A second mission is assisting in development of Latin American air forces, helping them to achieve the self-sufficiency necessary for their participation in defense of the Western Hemisphere.

USAFSO is further assigned the command of military groups in Argentina, Chile, Colombia, Peru and Uruguay, providing assistance in carrying out the Latin American Military Assistance Program, maintaining readiness for air defense of the Canal Zone and conducting search and rescue operations in the Southern Command area.

Headquartered at Albrook AFB, Canal Zone, USAFSO has an area of responsibility roughly two and a half times the size of the continental United States. For training of Latin American forces in counter-guerrilla and civic action activities, USAFSO has the 605th Air Commando Squadron at Howard AFB, Canal Zone, which also sends mobile training teams into Central and South American countries. Another element of the training program is introducing USAF standards of technical competence to Latin American air forces; for this purpose USAFSO operates the USAF School for Latin America at Albrook AFB. The school provides training in 23 different subjects, taught in Spanish by bilingual USAF instructors, to about 500 Latin American officers and airmen a year.

Also at Albrook AFB is the USAF Tropic Survival School, which trains, in addition to USAF flying personnel, airmen of the U.S. Army, Navy and Marine Corps, other Federal agencies, the Latin American air forces and astronauts of the National Aeronautics and Space Administration. Such training has proved so valuable that similar schools have been established in Argentina, Colombia and Peru.

For the command's mission of providing airlift for contingency operations, USAFSO operates a small fleet of Lockheed C-130 and C-118 transports based at Howard AFB. Should the need arise for additional airlift, planes would be provided by MATS or the U.S. Strike Command. Similarly, in an emergency USAFSO forces would be augmented by aircraft and personnel from Air Defense Command and Tactical Air Command.

*GOOD OLE PEMMICAN, BY WOODI ISHMAEL. Artist Ishmael drew on first-hand knowledge for his representative view of the Air Force Tropical Survival School in the Canal Zone.*

238

FORCE MISSION PLANE OVER ECUADOR, BY JOHN PIKE.

JUNGLE RESCUE IN ECUADOR, BY JOHN PIKE.

## Continental Air Command

From its headquarters at Robins AFB, Georgia, the Continental Air Command directs the Air Force Reserve program, a function which involves command, operational control, training and inspection of AFR units and individual reservists who are not part of an organized unit.

One of many additional CONAC assignments is supervision of the Civil Air Patrol, a national organization and an auxiliary of the Air Force, which flies more than half of all the inland search hours flown in the United States, maintains a communications network of about 14,500 stations and conducts an aerospace education and youth training program. CAP has some 82,000 adult and cadet members.

Among other special activities of the command are liaison with the Selective Service System; assisting other commands by recruiting reserve personnel to meet increased requirements; formulating USAF plans for provision of assistance in domestic and civil defense emergencies; representing the Air Force on Office of Civil Defense and Office of Emergency Planning Regional Boards; and supervising USAF cooperative activities with the Boy Scouts of America.

CONAC's major subdivisions are the Air Reserve Regions, of which there are six: the First, headquartered at Stewart AFB, New York; Second, Andrews AFB, Maryland; Third, Dobbins AFB, Georgia; Fourth, Randolph AFB, Texas; Fifth, Selfridge AFB, Michigan; and Sixth, Hamilton AFB, California.

The regions are further subdivided into 16 Air Reserve Sectors supervising non-flying units and other activities assigned to them.

CONAC's reserve unit complex includes 15 troop carrier wings with 45 groups, five air rescue squadrons, 24 mobile communications squadrons and detachments, 11 navigation training squadrons, 12 air terminal squadrons, one censorship squadron, one selective service squadron, 14 aeromedical evacuation units, 10 postal units, one USAF hospital, 21 medical service squadrons and 125 medical service flights.

*UNLOADING CONAC RESERVE C-119, BY WESLEY McKEOWN.*

*Headquarters Command and the Separate Operating Agencies*

Headquarters Command provides administrative support for some 12,000 Air Force personnel in more than 600 locations throughout the world, including those working with the Federal Aviation Agency, the National Aeronautics and Space Administration, the Defense Supply Agency, the Defense Intelligence Agency, Military Assistance Advisory Groups, Air Attache offices and the North Atlantic Treaty Organization. The command has its headquarters at Bolling AFB, Washington, D.C.; its structure includes the 1100th Air Base Wing at Bolling AFB and the 1001st ABW at nearby Andrews AFB. In addition to its administrative function, Headquarters Command provides aircraft for proficiency flying of all USAF personnel stationed in the Washington area, and it controls the activities of the USAF Band and the USAF Ceremonial Unit.

Among the USAF's ''separate operating agencies'' is the Air Force Accounting and Finance Center, located at Denver, Colorado, which administers about 1,300,000 allotments and 100,000 retired pay accounts and makes monthly financial status reports to a number of government agencies.

The Aeronautical Chart and Information Center, St. Louis, Missouri, in addition to its obvious mission of providing maps and charts, also services the USAF with graphic air target materials, terrain models, flight information publications and intelligence on air facilities, geodetic and geophysical data.

The Air Force Communications Service, Scott AFB, Illinois, maintains communications, air traffic control and air navigation services for the USAF and for other government and civilian agencies.

The Office of Aerospace Research, Washington, D.C., plans and manages the USAF basic research program and certain parts of the exploratory development program. Its objective is to pursue scientific knowledge and analyze advanced concepts which may permit the Air Force to develop new and superior weapon systems. OAS operates three major laboratories and a rocket research range, and administers contracts with industry, universities and research institutions.

The United States Air Force Security Service insures that information transmitted by electrical means is safeguarded en route. The agency's functions include analysis of USAF communications to determine the effectiveness of security measures in force and provision of cryptographic equipment and materials. Headquarters is at Kelly AFB, Texas.

*VAPOR TRAILS, BY RALPH ILIGAN.*

*Toward Tomorrow*

Says the USAF Chief of Staff, General John P. McConnell:

''The various forms of aggression which the Communists are able to employ, plus the small and unpredictable crises which result from today's situation of broadly diffused political power, call for the Air Force to maintain a force posture adequate for a broad range of tasks. This requirement can only be met with these capabilities:

''Strategic aerospace systems, manned and unmanned, capable of performing complementary missions because of the unique mission characteristics possessed by each; flexible, damage-limiting defensive weapon systems, capable of coping with the space-age threats posed by manned or unmanned enemy weapon systems; all-weather and night-capable reconnaissance vehicles that can collect accurate and comprehensive intelligence; tactical aircraft and missiles, equipped with either conventional or nuclear weapons, that can perform discriminating and selective tasks commensurate with military necessity; airlift capability to respond rapidly to emergencies and to add credibility to our contingency posture; and, lastly, command and control networks that will provide flexible, rugged and mobile communications that can operate in any environment.''

The Air Force is achieving these capabilities with careful expenditure of its resources, the most economical use of men, money and materiel. It has built the mightiest aerospace force ever assembled by any nation. But it is not enough to provide for today. The USAF must also maintain ''aerospace supremacy'' in the years to come, in an atmosphere of leapfrogging technology that brings rapid obsolescence to the most advanced weapon systems.

Toward that end, the Air Force is conducting a broad program of research and development that delves into all the areas of capability outlined by General McConnell. At the same time, the extensive educational system is bringing forth new leaders, tomorrow's additions to the roster which includes such illustrious names as Chandler, Lahm and Foulois, Rickenbacker, Mitchell and Doolittle, Arnold, Spaatz, Vandenberg, Twining, White, LeMay and McConnell.

Six decades of history, rich in tradition and accomplishment, lend confidence that the future of the United States Air Force will be as distinguished as its past.

GRADUATION DAY AT THE AIR FORCE ACADEMY, BY NORMAN
NICHOLSON. *The transition from cadet to officer, the start of a
new career, symbolizes the future of the Air Force.*

# Biographies

AL AVISON operates an art studio which services advertising agencies, magazines and other clients, and handles reenlistment programs for the military. A veteran of the Pacific area during World War II, he was Head of the Pictures and Art Section, Army General Headquarters, Tokyo, after the war. Later, he took three years of advanced study at Pratt Institute. He is a member of the Society of Illustrators of New York.

GEORGE C. BALES, born in Dane, Indiana, served on active duty with the USAF as Director of Art from 1954 until his retirement in 1963. A graduate of the University of Illinois, he worked under Robert Phillip at that institution and studied portrait painting in Los Angeles under the late Will Foster and in New York under Robert Brackman. A former artist with Walt Disney Studios, he is a member of the Society of Illustrators of New York.

JAMES BAMA was born in New York City, studied at the Art Students League and in World War II served in the Army Air Forces. He has illustrated accounts with Ford, Goodyear, General Electric, RCA Television, Chevrolet and the Pennsylvania Railroad and has done many covers for children's books. Bama has specialized in family type illustrations and character studies.

CHARLES BASKERVILLE, a native of North Carolina, studied at Cornell University, the Art Students League in New York and the Academie Julien in Paris. He is one of the nation's leading portrait painters and a member of the American Society of Mural Painters and the American Artists Professional League. He has exhibited at the Whitney Museum of Modern Art, the Carnegie Institute of Technology, the Metropolitan Museum of Art, the National Gallery of Art and the Corcoran Gallery in Washington, D.C.

C. C. BEALL started his career in the commercial art field in the early part of the century. After World War I, his illustrations appeared in many leading magazines. In 1936, he became art director for the National Democratic Committee. During World War II, he made numerous posters for the government; his best known one, "Raising the Flag at Iwo" has been reprinted 57,000,000 times. At the end of World War II, when he was in the Philippines and Japan, he painted "Surrender," which was later presented to President Truman.

FRANCIS HENRY BEAUGUREAU, originally from Chicago, studied at Mizen Academy and the Art Institute of Chicago. Winner of the Kautsky Memorial and American Watercolor Society awards, his paintings have been exhibited in such places as the Frye (Seattle) Museum of Art, the Corcoran Gallery of Art, the American Watercolor Society, the Phoenix Watercolor Exhibition, the Arizona State Fair and the University of Arizona. He is a member of the American Watercolor Society and the Philadelphia Watercolor Club.

BILL BENDER is a native of El Segundo, California. He works entirely in the fine arts field through galleries and for private clientele. His paintings hang in the Desert-Southwest Art Gallery, Palm Desert, California; O'Brien's Art Emporium, Scottsdale, Arizona; and the Grand Central Galleries in New York. He exhibits in several one-man shows each year. Bender is an Associate Fellow, American Institute of Fine Arts, and a member of the Society of Illustrators.

FRANK E. BERESFORD was born in Derby, England, 30 August, 1881. He attended the Derby School of Art and earned a Master's Certificate at the age of eighteen. In 1900, he studied at St. John's Wood School of Art in London and then the Royal Academy until 1906. Under the sponsorship of John Sargant, his first picture was hung in the Royal Academy. He is a member of the United Society of Artists and the Society of Aviation Artists, and he has painted portraits of many members of the Royal Family. Mr. Bereford now lives in Sussex, England.

ROY BESSER studied art at the Graphic Sketch Club of Philadelphia. After working for a Philadelphia agency on illustrations for national advertising, he moved to New York, where he did editorial illustrations for the *Saturday Evening Post,* Street and Smith publications, *Bluebook Magazine, Reader's Digest, Field and Stream* and other magazines. Besser is a nationally known photographer as well as an artist. He is a member of the Society of Illustrators of Los Angeles.

NEIL BOYLE, a native Canadian, studied at the Banff School of Fine Art in Alberta, the Art Center School and Chouinard Art Institute of Los Angeles. He has used unusual techniques, including line and wash, casein and charcoal, in rendering his paintings. Both the New York Society of Illustrators and the Los Angeles Society have honored him with meritorious awards.

GERALD BROCKHURST, an Englishmen and a distinguished United Kingdom painter, did the portrait of General H. H. Arnold. This work was included in a New York exhibition called ''Portraits in Review.''

CARL BROEMEL, born in Ohio, studied at the Cleveland School of Art, National Academy in New York, the Art Students League in New York, and at the Royal Academy in Munich. Broemel has been doing fine arts painting and illustrating since 1925, has received five prize awards at the Cleveland Museum of Art and has had eleven one-man exhibits. As an illustrator, his work is chiefly in architectural subjects and landscapes. He is a former president of the New York Artists' Guild and Cleveland Society of Artists.

MARBURY HILL BROWN is a graduate of Jepson Art Institute and the Kansas City Art Institute. He has won a number of art prizes and his work has been shown in the collections of the Houston Museum of Fine Art, the Dallas Museum of Fine Art and the Dallas Collection of Edward Marcus. His commercial illustrations have appeared in many national magazines. He is a member of the Society of Illustrators of New York and the Texas Watercolor Society.

REYNOLD BROWN, of Los Angeles, California, attended Otis Art Institute there. His illustrations have appeared in a number of national magazines and his paintings hang in the Laguna Beach Gallery and the Westchester Gallery. He is a member of the American Institute of Fine Arts, the Laguna Art Club and the Society of Illustrators of Los Angeles, and he serves on the staff of the Art Center School of Los Angeles.

LYNN BUCKHAM was born in Minnesota and studied at the Minneapolis School of Art and the American Academy of Art in Chicago. He served four and a half years in the Army. His illustrations have appeared in *Cosmopolitan, Good Housekeeping, Saturday Evening Post, Red Book, McCall's* and other magazines.

AL BUELL is a native of Kansas who attended the Chicago Art Institute and began his career in New York City, then moved to Chicago and, finally, to Sarasota, Florida. He has illustrated for most of the important national magazines and his advertising work includes Ford Motor Company, Coca-Cola, and Brown and Bigelow.

PAUL CALLE attended Pratt Institute in Hoboken, New Jersey, and majored in illustration. He has had a distinguished career in illustrating for a number of major magazines, including *National Geographic.*

COLLIN BRUCE CAMPBELL was born in St. Charles, Michigan, and studied art in California and Paris. He served with the Navy in both the Atlantic and Pacific during World War II, worked in Spain and then traveled to Japan and Korea for the Air Force Art Program. He is now a member of the Walt Disney staff.

JOSEPH CLEARY, from Long Beach, California, was educated at San Francisco State College, California College of Arts and Crafts and Mills College. He has paintings in the galleries of the Legion of Honor, San Francisco Museum of Art, Oakland Museum of Art and De Young Museum. His memberships include the Society of Illustrators of San Francisco, East Bay Art Association and the Bohemian Club.

CHET COLLOM, a native of Glendale, California, attended the School of Allied Art there and the Chouinard Art Institute in Los Angeles. He has served as treasurer of the Society of Illustrators of Los Angeles and his paintings have been on exhibition at the Los Angeles Art Association.

MARIO COOPER, born of American parents in Mexico City, received his training at Otis Art Institute, Chouinard Art Institute, Grand Central School of Art and Columbia University. He has taught at Chouinard and Columbia, and at Pratt Institute. Cooper's work is widely exhibited in leading museums throughout the country. He is a member and former president of the Audubon Society and a member of the Society of Illustrators and the American Watercolor Society.

DONALD V. CROWLEY, originally from Redlands, California, has done illustrative work for a number of advertising agencies, book and magazine publishers and commercial organizations. His paintings have been shown in New York, San Francisco and Los Angeles, and he is a member of the Society of Illustrators of New York.

AL DEMPSTER, born July 1911 in Atlantic City, New Jersey, came to Los Angeles in 1918 and later studied at the Art Center School. He has exhibited at the Disney Library, Santa Paula, Tarzana, Woodland Hills and Encino and is represented in private collections in the Southwest, Washington and Peru. Dempster is a member of the Society of Illustrators of Los Angeles.

DEAN ELLIS is a native of Detroit, Michigan. He trained for four years at the Cleveland Institute of Art and one year at Boston Museum School of Fine Arts. He has done illustrations for many industrial firms, and his collections are in the Cleveland Museum of Art, Akron Art Institute, Columbus Art Museum, University of Illinois, Colgate University and Atlanta Art Museum; they are also in the Academy of Arts and Letters, State Museum of Illinois, Butler Art Institute. Norton Gallery, and the Museum of Fine Arts.

HENRI FARRÉ, 1871–1934, came from Foix, France. He graduated from L'Ecole Des Beaux Arts and, at twenty-six, held his first exhibition at the Salon Des Artistes Francais. His paintings now hang in the Musee Des Invalides and other French national museums. At the outbreak of World War I, Farré volunteered his services to his country. He was given the rank of observer-bombardier and assigned to a Groupe D'Escadrille de Bombardment. One of his special missions was to record the combat, bombing, reconnaissance and aerial activities of the early days of military aviation. The Farré collection was presented to the USAF through the generosity of Mr. Laurance S. Rockefeller.

DEAN (WILLIAM) FAUSETT, born in Price, Utah, studied at Brigham Young University and the Colorado Springs Fine Art Center. He is a member of the National Society of Miniature Painters and the Southern Vermont Art Association. His work is represented in the Metropolitan Museum of Art, Museum of Modern Art, the University of Arizona, The White House, Williams College, Princeton University, the American Academy of Arts and Letters, and other collections. Fausett has exhibited at the Whitney Museum of American Art, Carnegie Institute, Art Institute of Chicago, Corcoran Gallery of Art, National Academy of Design and the Metropolitan Museum of Art.

NICOLAI FECHIN, whose career began as a peasant woodcarver, continued by studying drawings and painting under the great realist painter, Repine. By 1914 his paintings of people, flowers and landscapes were valued throughout Europe and were becoming known in the United States. By the time World War I began, Mr. Fechin had won fame in his native Russia, the Prix de Rome from the Imperial Academy and gold medals in Petrograd, Vienna and Prague. War and Revolution put an end to his first career, and he began a new one on this continent when he was 33. It has been said that he brought to America art gifts that are rare in its history. His drawing showed a deep empathy with all that is untamed and freedom-loving in mankind. At the time of his death he was, as throughout most of his life, hard at work painting.

KEITH FERRIS was born in Honolulu, Hawaii, the son of a retired USAF colonel. He attended Texas A&M College, George Washington University and the Corcoran School of Art in Washington, D.C., starting his art career as illustrator in the USAF with Air Force Training Publications at Randolph Air Force Base, Texas. He studied in Europe, then moved to New York in 1956 to work as an illustrator specializing in aviation and aerospace industrial art. He is a member of the New York Society of Illustrators.

251

LOREN RUSSELL FISHER was a student at the John Herron Art School in Indianapolis for four years. In 1940, at the age of 27, he was recipient of the John H. Lazarus Fellowship provided by the Metropolitan Museum of Art. This painting fellowship to the American Academy in Rome was awarded him on the basis of his painting "Chicken Market." Later, he was active in the China-Burma theater of World War II, painting some of the scenes now in the Air Force Art Collection.

STANLEY W. GALLI studied at the California School of Fine Arts in his native San Francisco. He has exhibited in San Francisco galleries for a period of 20 years. He is a member of the San Francisco Art Association, Society of Designers and Illustrators, San Francisco, and the Society of Illustrators, New York.

NIXON GALLOWAY's work has been shown at exhibitions of the Art Directors' Club, the Santa Monica Library, the Los Angeles County Museum and the Palos Verdes Art Gallery. A member of the Society of Illustrators of Los Angeles, Galloway attended Art Center School in Los Angeles and Famous Artists' School in Connecticut.

ROBERT GEISSMANN is the present Air Force Chairman, USAF Documentary Art Program. He acts as liaison between the Air Force and the Society of Illustrators of New York. Since 1954, his interest and enthusiasm have been instrumental in the development of a contemporary collection of approximately 500 paintings covering world-wide activities of the Air Force. He was born at New Washington, Ohio, and attended schools in Mansfield and Warren, Ohio. He received art and academic training at Ohio State University. During World War II, he was the art director for the Army Air Forces Combat Film Unit, recording air campaigns in every theater of operation, and also for the Air Force Weekly Digest of combat films.

FRANK GERMAIN comes from Gerber, California. His paintings have appeared in the Los Angeles County Museum, and he has done illustrations for many advertising companies. He is a member of the Society of Illustrators of Los Angeles.

RICHARD GREEN was born in East Liverpool, Ohio, and educated at Ohio State University. During World War II, he served with the Office of Strategic Services as gunnery officer and as an artist for the Navy. He has done illustrations for *Esquire, Good Housekeeping, Reader's Digest* and many other magazines and advertising work for many commercial firms. He is a member of the Society of Illustrators of New York and Westport Artists of Connecticut.

BOB GREENBERG, a resident of Los Angeles since 1945, was born in Chicago and attended Chicago Academy of Art and Chouinard Art Institute. In 1960 he graduated from the University of California at Los Angeles with a Master of Arts degree in painting. He has worked as an advertising artist, art director and art instructor and is currently teaching painting and drawing.

EARL G. GROSS, born in Pittsburgh, Pennsylvania, studied at Westminster College and graduated from Carnegie Institute of Technology. Gross has done illustrations for many magazines, notably *Cosmopolitan*; he has had one-man shows in Macbeth Galleries of New York, Associated Artists, New York and the Art Institute of Chicago. He is a member of the American Watercolor Society and the Artists Guild, Chicago.

JOHN GROTH, born in Chicago, studied at the Chicago Art Institute and the Art Students League of New York. He has exhibited in the major East Coast museums, was a war correspondent for the Chicago Sun and American Legion Magazine during World War II, and currently illustrates for a number of American magazines. He wrote and illustrated the book *Studio Asia*, covering the United Nations troops in Korea, and he has won many awards in art exhibits. His one-man shows have been seen at the Library of Congress, Grand Central Ferargil Galleries and Art Students League of New York. He has permanent collections in the Museum of Modern Art and Metropolitan, New York, the Library of Congress and the Chicago Art Institute. Groth is a member of the Society of Illustrators, American Society of Etchers, Philadelphia Society of Etchers and the Chicago Society of Etchers.

DAVID HALL is a West Coast artist living in the Los Angeles area where, for many years, he has been associated with the film industry.

ROBERT HANDVILLE, of Patterson, New Jersey, attended Albright College and Pratt Institute. A veteran of both World War II and Korea, he has done advertising art for a number of commercial firms and his work has also appeared in *Time, Life* and the *Saturday Evening Post*. He is a member of the American Watercolor Society and the Society of Illustrators of New York.

LLOYD F. HARTING, born in Little Falls, Minnesota, studied at Minneapolis School of Fine Arts, Chicago Art Institute and Grand Central Art School of New York. For 30 years he was an illustrator for Brown & Bigelow, St. Paul, Minnesota, and he has since worked for Walt Disney Studios and 20th Century Fox. He is a member of the Society of Illustrators of Los Angeles.

PETER HURD was born in Roswell, New Mexico, 22 February, 1904. He studied at Pennsylvania Academy of Fine Arts and with N. C. Wyeth. Mr. Hurd is distinguished for his portraiture and is well-known for his paintings of the Southwest. His paintings hang in William Rockhill Nelson Gallery, Herron Art Institute, Metropolitan Museum of Art, Brooklyn Museum, and in European museums as well. Permanently housed in Roswell Museum is a collection of his paintings, drawings and lithographs.

RALPH ILIGAN, 1893–1960, attended school in New York, studied under several well-known artists and attended the Pratt Institute and the Art Students League. His work hangs in many galleries and museums throughout the country. For 11 years he taught at the Industrial School of Art in New York City. Part of his time was devoted to private tutoring. He was a member of the Society of Illustrators of New York, of the Artists and Writers and the Salmagundi clubs.

WOODI ISHMAEL, born in Lewis County, Kentucky, graduated from the Cleveland School of Art in 1936 and later studied under Lewis Daniels in New York City. His work has appeared in the Cleveland Museum of Art, the Denver Art Museum, the Smithsonian Institution and the Westchester County Annual Art Show in New York, and has been on view in the art galleries of many national colleges and universities. A member of the Society of Illustrators in New York, he exhibits at the Society's shows and at the Art Directors Club of New York. Ishmael has depicted many well-known individuals through the syndicated Associated Press ''Power of Faith'' column, which appears in more than 100 national newspapers each week.

HARVEY KIDDER, a member of the Society of Illustrators of New York, is a graduate of Boston Art School. He illustrates for a number of magazines, publishing companies and industrial organizations, and he won first prize (watercolor) in the Manhattan Savings Bank Exhibition of 1963.

WARREN KING is a graduate of Fordham University, from which he received a Bachelor of Science degree in 1938, and where he was sports cartoonist and art editor of the school paper. He studied art at the Grand Central School in New York and at the Phoenix Art Institute and later taught art at Fordham University. One of Mr. King's cartoons won the Freedom Foundation Award in 1953. He has illustrated book and magazine covers and handled movie illustrations for Warner Brothers Studios.

DAVID KLEIN was born in El Paso, Texas, and he studied for five years at the Art Center School in Los Angeles. He is a member of the Society of Illustrators of New York and his paintings have been exhibited at the Los Angeles County Museum and the Museum of Modern Art.

SANDOR KLEIN maintains studios in New York City and Los Angeles and has had a thorough training in portraiture. His schools include the National Academy of Design in New York City, the Academie Julien in Paris, and others in Germany, Austria and Hungary. His honors include a Pulitzer Prize and a Fellowship to the American Academy in Rome, Italy, in 1932.

CLAYTON KNIGHT, a well-known artist and illustrator, was a pilot in World War I. Many of his paintings are in private collections, and he has been widely exhibited.

ALEXANDER KORTNER, born in Pittsburgh, Pennsylvania attended the Art Institute of Pittsburgh, Art Institute of Chicago, National Art Academy and the American Art Academy. He has won many awards in exhibitions in the American Watercolor Society, Society of Illustrators, Allied Artists, Fairfield (Connecticut) Watercolor Group, Hudson Valley Art Association and the Greenwich (Connecticut) Art Society.

CHARLES J. KUDERNA is a native of Chicago, Illinois. He attended the Chicago Art Institute, the Chicago Academy of Arts and George Washington University. His paintings hang in a number of galleries and he has been exhibited in the New York Art Directors' Club, Chicago Art Directors' Club and Los Angeles Art Directors' Club annual exhibitions. He is a member of the Society of Illustrators of Los Angeles and on the faculty of Chouinard Art Institute.

ROBERT H. LAESSIG, born in West New York, New Jersey, attended Textile Design School in Plauen, Germany for five years and studied at the Art Students League in New York City under Bernard Klonis. Laessig won prizes at Knickerbocker Artists Show in New York City; the Philadelphia Watercolor Show; Mead Shaiver, Chicago, and Chautauqua, New York. He is a member of the American Watercolor Society and an associate member in the National Academy of Design and the National Society of Painters in Casein.

JOHN LAVALLE is a native of Nahant, Massachusetts. He studied at Harvard, the Boston Museum of Fine Arts, the Academie Julien in Paris, and under a number of well-known artists, including Philip Hale and Jean Francis Auburtin of Paris. Lavalle is a member of the Guild of Boston Artists, American Watercolor Society, the Boston Society of Watercolor Painters, and the Copely Society. His works hang in the Boston Museum of Fine Arts; Harvard University; the Columbia University Museum; Amherst College Museum; and he has been exhibited at the Corcoran Gallery of Art, the Pennsylvania Academy of Fine Arts and the Carnegie Institute.

ROBERT LAVIN, of New York City, graduated from City College there and attended the National Academy Art School. During World War II, as a Marine captain, he piloted a Corsair in the Pacific theater. He has exhibited in the National Academy show, Audubon Society show and others.

JACK LEVINE, born in Boston, Massachusetts, is a member of the American Academy of Arts and Sciences and the National Institute of Arts and Letters. His works hang in the Metropolitan Museum of Art; the Museum of Modern Art; the University of Nebraska; Portland (Oregon) Museum; the Walker Art Center and the University of Arizona. Levine has held exhibitions in the Carnegie Institution, the Whitney Museum of American Art, and the Art Institute of Chicago.

MILTON MARX, a native of Chicago, graduated from the University of Illinois as a landscape architect. His background includes extensive work in portraits and water colors and, from 1957 on, an active career in commercial art. He exhibited an extensive collection of water colors, painted in Greece, at the Museum of the City of New York.

TRAN MAWICKE was educated at St. Thomas Military Academy, the Chicago Art Institute and the American Academy of Art. A free lance artist in New York, he has representation in various museums and private collections and has executed numerous portrait commissions. Mawicke is a member of the American Watercolor Society, the Salmagundi Club and the Society of Illustrators of New York.

ROBERT T. McCALL began his formal art training at the Columbus (Ohio) Fine Arts School through a scholarship won during his senior year in high school; later he studied at the Art Institute of Chicago. During World War II, he was a bombardier with the Army Air Forces. Following his military service, he returned to Chicago in 1945 where he worked as an illustrator for advertising agencies and publishing houses. McCall enjoys painting all subjects, but his first love is airplanes and he is internationally known for his aircraft art.

GERALD McCONNELL was born in West Orange, New Jersey, and in New York City he studied at the Art Students League under Frank J. Reilly and is a member of the Society of Illustrators there. His work has appeared in such magazines as *Motor, Columbia,* and *Bowling*; in publications of Golden Books, Simon and Schuster, American Books and on pocketbook covers for Avon, Ace, Dell and others.

JOHN T. McCOY has a unique background in Air Force lore. He became an aviation devotee in high school and in 1926 learned to fly in a Curtiss Jenny. In World War II he was assigned to the Air Force Historical Office and produced the official *Pictorial History of the Army Air Forces.*

WESLEY B. McKEOWN is a native of Jersey City, New Jersey, and he attended the Newark School of Fine and Industrial Arts. He has illustrated for the *Reader's Digest*; American Book Co.; D. C. Heath Co.; Holt, Rinehart, Winston; McCall Corp., *Bluebook Magazine*; Redbook Promo.; Texaco Corp.; MacFadden-Bartell; SAGA; Climax Magazines; *Family Weekly*; Simmons-Boadman Publishing Co.; Scholastic Publications; Grolier Society; New Jersey Bell Telephone; and many agencies and studios in the New York area. He is represented in many private collections and he is a member of the Society of Illustrators of New York.

SAM McKIM was born in North Vancouver, British Columbia. He graduated from the Art Center School, Los Angeles, and from Chouinard Art Institute of Los Angeles. He prepared illustrations for Walt Disney publications and he was designer and sketch-artist on a number of Disneyland attractions. He had similar assignments at the 1964 World's Fair in New York. A motion picture actor since 1935, he is a member of the Society of Illustrators of Los Angeles and the Motion Picture Illustrators.

SI MEZEROW received his technical training at the Art Students League and Grand Central School of Art in New York City. He is nationally known as an illustrator for the McFadden publications, the Bulova Watch Co., the J. R. Wood Co., General Electric, The Martin Company and other firms. Serving with the Navy in 1944–45, Mr. Mezerow participated in the Normandy invasion and was later assigned to duty with the Army as Pictorial Recorder of Operations in the European Theater. In addition to advertising and story illustration, Mr. Mezerow's present schedule includes teaching at the Chouinard Art Institute in Los Angeles.

HERB MOTT, born in Passaic, New Jersey, attended the New York Phoenix School of Design. During World War II, he was in the Visual Training Aids Department of the Army Air Forces. His commercial work includes such clients as Goodyear Tire and Rubber, General Motors, RCA Communications and many others; his illustrations have appeared in *Argosy, Saga, American Legion, Elks Magazine* and *Railroad Magazine*.

ALFRED MUENCHEN, originally from Cincinnati, Ohio, attended Carnegie Tech Art School and the Chicago Art Institute. His illustrations have appeared in the *Saturday Evening Post, Life, Collier's, American, Field and Stream* and *Time*, and his paintings have been shown at the Society of Illustrators in New York. He is a member of the Silvermine Guild of Artists, in Connecticut, and the Society of Illustrators of New York.

NORMAN NICHOLSON was born in San Francisco, Calitornia, and he attended the Art Center School of Los Angeles. For six years he has been producing illustrations for major industrial accounts in western United States. His paintings are on display in the Society of Illustrator shows in New York, Los Angeles and San Francisco, as well as in many private collections throughout the United States, and he is a member of the Society of Illustrators of San Francisco.

ROBERT PHILLIP, a native New Yorker, studied at the Art Students League and the National Academy of Design. He is a member of the National Academy of Design and the Lotos Club. Phillip has won many awards and his work hangs in the Whitney Museum of American Art, Brooklyn Museum, Fine Art Museum of Houston, Corcoran Gallery of Art, Norton Gallery of Art, High Museum of Art, IBM, Davenport Municipal Art Gallery, Dallas Museum, University of Arizona, and the Joslyn Art Museum.

BARYE W. PHILLIPS took his training at the National Academy of Design and the Art Students League. Prior to 1943, he worked for newspapers and motion picture companies; during the war years, he served as an art director in the Army. Since the war, he has been engaged in editorial art. Phillips is a member of the Salmagundi Club and the Society of Illustrators.

JOHN PIKE, born at Woodstock, New York, has had seventeen one-man exhibitions and has watercolors in many public and private collections. His awards include the American Watercolor Society, Salmagundi Black and White prize and National Academy Halgarten Prize; he has illustrated covers for *Collier's, Life, Fortune* and *Reader's Digest.* Pike is a member of the National Academy of Design, American Watercolor Society, Salmagundi Club, Woodstock Art Association, Philadelphia Watercolor Club and the Society of Illustrators.

OGDEN PLEISSNER of Brooklyn, New York, studied at the Art Students League in New York. He holds membership in the National Arts Club, the Century Association and the Art Students League. His paintings hang in the Brooklyn Museum, Davenport Municipal Art Gallery, Lyman Allyn Museum, the University of Georgia, the Philbrook Art Center, the University of Maine, the Colby College, IBM, the Pentagon, the Massachusetts Institute of Technology, the Chrysler Collection and the University of Vermont.

ROBERT POOLE, born in Tacoma, Washington, attended Cornish Art School, Seattle; the Art Center in Los Angeles; Chouinard Art School, Los Angeles; and Pasadena School of Art. He is a member of the Society of Illustrators of Los Angeles.

RAY PROHASKA came to America from Austria-Hungary and graduated from the California School of Fine Arts, San Francisco. An illustrator for many national magazines, he has won a number of art awards and is widely exhibited. He is a member of the Artists and Writers Club and the Society of Illustrators of New York.

NOEL QUINN is a native of Pawtucket, Rhode Island. After graduation from the Rhode Island School of Design in 1936, he went to France on a fellowship, later studying in Italy, Germany and the Near East. He worked as Art Director in the Paris office of the J. Walter Thompson Advertising Agency, but with the outbreak of the war, he returned to the United States to work as an artist in the motion picture industry. Since 1946, he has devoted almost full time to fine arts. Quinn is represented in many private collections in Europe and the United States and has received many awards. He is a member of the American Watercolor Society, the Philadelphia Watercolor Club, the California Watercolor Society, Society of Motion Picture Illustrators and the National Society of Art Directors (Los Angeles Chapter), and the Society of Illustrators, Los Angeles.

WALTER RICHARDS, born in Penfield, Ohio, studied at the Cleveland School of Art. He does art work for General Motors, U.S. Steel, General Electric and several aviation companies and he has had work in many of the popular magazines. He has exhibited at the Cleveland Museum of Art; Art Institute, Chicago; Pennsylvania Academy of Fine Arts; the Brooklyn Museum; Metropolitan Museum and the Whitney Museum. Richards has won numerous awards in New York City exhibitions and he is considered one of the top lithographers in America.

ART RILEY, active for 30 years in art work, photography and the motion picture business, is a graduate of the Art Center School of Los Angeles. He has been widely exhibited and his illustrations have appeared in a number of American magazines. He is a member of the Laguna Beach (California) Art Association.

HARRY J. SCHAARE was born in Jamaica, New York. He attended New York University School of Architecture for one year and Pratt Institute for three years, graduating from the School of Illustration in 1947. His illustrations appear in Bantam Books, Dell Books, 20th Century Fox, United Artists Films; *Saturday Evening Post, True, Argosy, Saga,* Doubleday Publishing Co., Holt, Rinehart, Winston Publishing Co., Hearst Publishing Co., and Grosset & Dunlap. His portrait of Ernie Pyle is in Indianapolis War Memorial. He is a member of the Society of Illustrators of New York and the Artists and Writers Association.

JOHN SCOTT is a former combat artist who was inducted into the Army Engineers in April, 1942, and transferred to *Yank Magazine* as an artist-correspondent, serving in that capacity during 1943–44.

CARL SETTERBERG is an illustrator for a wide variety of American and European magazines. Born in Las Animas, Colorado, he studied in Chicago at the Art Institute and the Academy of Fine Art. He is a member of the Society of Illustrators and the American Watercolor Society and his work is represented in the permanent collections of the Air Force Academy, the Columbus (Georgia) Museum and McChord Air Force Base.

GEORGE A. SHEALY, born in Chicago, Illinois, won a scholarship to Indiana University in 1927–28 then spent three years at the Chicago Art Institute where he studied drawing, painting and illustrating. He studied five summers at Oxbow Summer School of Painting, Saugatuck, Michigan; studied with John Norton in his mural studio; taught art at Todd School for Boys, Woodstock, Illinois; designed and built sets for summer theater with Orson Welles and Hilton Edwards of the Gate Theatre, Dublin; and taught at St. Ambrose College, Davenport, Iowa. He was in the Army Combat Engineers in World War II and at the request of the Office of War Information he was sent to London to be art director on publications. Shealy set up his own studio in 1950 as a free lance art director and illustrator and later became Head of the Department of Art, Queens College, Charlotte, North Carolina.

HARRISON STANDLEY was born in San Francisco in 1916 and graduated from Stanford University. He attended Pomona College, the Art Center School in Los Angeles, and the Academie de la Grande Chaumière of Paris. As a Tech/Sgt in the Air Corps during World War II, he was stationed in Iceland, England and France. After the war he returned to Paris, married a French girl and continued his fine arts career.

THOMAS EDGAR STEPHENS was born in Cardiff, South Wales, and he took his training at Cardiff University School of Fine Arts, Heatherly School in London and the Academie Julien in Paris. His work has been exhibited in a great many galleries, among them the White House, the National Gallery of Art, the Legion of Honor Gallery in Paris and the Eisenhower Library. He is a member of the Savage Club (London), the Salmagundi Club and the National Arts Club.

PAUL TREBILCOCK, a native of Chicago, studied at the University of Illinois, the Art Institute of Chicago and in Europe. He has won a number of art awards and his work is widely exhibited. He is a member of the National Academy of Design, the Chicago Art Club, the Century Association and the Chelsea Art Culb of London.

THORNTON UTZ was born in Memphis, Tennessee. He is an advertising, story and cover illustrator who took his training at the American Academy of Art and later served as an illustration instructor at the Art Institute in Chicago. His work has appeared in the *Saturday Evening Post, Cosmopolitan* and *McCall's*, among other magazines.

ELIN WAITE, a native of Los Angeles, attended Jepson Art Institute, California School of Art and is also a graduate of Chouinard Art Institute. Currently working for *Westways Magazine*, she is also public relations staff artist for the Automobile Club of Southern California. She has free-lanced editorial and advertising illustrations, package and display designs, slide films and serigraphs. Her drawings have been exhibited in the California State Fair in Sarcamento and in several Los Angeles shows, and her serigraphs have been on display in the Library of Congress. Miss Waite is a member of the Society of Illustrators of Los Angeles.

ROBERT O. WATKINS has the distinction of being a self-trained artist. He worked for the Civilian Conservation Corps doing design and taught military science and tactics at the Agricultural and Technical College in Greensboro, North Carolina. In 1954, he had a one-man show at Bennett College in Greensboro. Watkins' interest in aviation, which has led to his participation in the Air Force Art Program, started when his family lived close to Wright Field in Ohio.

REN WICKS, born in Syracuse, New York, took his training at Massachusetts School of Art in Boston; Cornish School of Art in Seattle; the Art Center School, Los Angeles; and Kann Institute of Art, Los Angeles. He has illustrated for a wide variety of magazines, his work hangs in the Washington Art Museum, Seattle, and he has won awards in a number of major art competitions. He is a member of the Societies of Illustrators of New York and Los Angeles.